READING THE HIDDEN COMMUNICATIONS AROUND YOU

A Guide to Reading the Body Language of Customers and Colleagues

Anne E. Beall, PhD

READING THE HIDDEN COMMUNICATIONS AROUND YOU: A Guide to Reading the Body Language of Customers and Colleagues

Copyright © 2019 by Beall Research, Inc.

Cover Designed by Anne E. Beall

ISBN: 9781093275292

For my parents.

In honor of my mother and in memory of my father

Contents

PREFACE

I think most of us are intrigued by the idea of reading body language. The idea that we can understand a secret language and discern the inner thoughts of others is very appealing. I've been intrigued with this idea ever since I was a teenager. My interest in reading people led me to study psychology in college and eventually to earn a PhD in social psychology from Yale University. While I was in graduate school, I studied nonverbal communication and became familiar with the large volume of research in this area. What I learned was amazing. People express many of their thoughts and feelings without uttering a word.

When I finished graduate school, I decided to pursue a career in the business world. I was eager to use my psychological training to solve real-world problems and to help people. I ended up working in a top consulting firm, Boston Consulting Group (BCG), doing marketing research to help businesses respond intelligently to their markets. I spent a lot of time interviewing and observing research respondents, and a lot of time observing my colleagues. Knowing the intricacies of nonverbal behavior helped me to *see* what was often unsaid. I noticed, however, that many of my colleagues didn't have this skill, and I wanted to help them.

I approached the training department of BCG and suggested that I teach a course on how to read nonverbal communications. They thought it was a great idea and I went to work. I scoured all the books on body language to prepare. I assumed that the most widely-read books were based on the large body of academic research. I was wrong. The books stated overly simplistic rules about reading others, and in some cases, things that were completely incorrect. I decided to go back to my graduate training and created PERCEIVE, which is a straightforward way of decoding all the major areas of nonverbal communication. The course was a hit, and several people who left the firm asked me to teach the same class to their companies. When I began my own firm, Beall Research Inc., body-language training was one of our major offerings.

We don't do many of those trainings any more but the need for understanding nonverbal communication of customers and colleagues has never been greater. We live in a world where being able to understand one another is paramount and even more important as we've become increasingly electronic in our communications. When we have the opportunity to read one another through our voices or when we're in person, it behooves us to do it well. And there is a lot of evidence that demonstrates that those who read the body language of their colleagues and customers are more successful.

It's my passion for this area that drove me to write this book. I want to share PERCEIVE with as many people as I can. Unlike other books on reading body language, this one is based on solid academic research. It's not my opinion—it's grounded entirely on science. And it's useful. I use it all the time when interacting with customers and colleagues, and I've been able to have much greater influence in these interactions as a result. I wrote this book for people who have to read customers or colleagues—that's pretty much anyone who has a job. Throughout the book I share examples of how people can use these skills in a variety of professional situations. Regardless of what type of job you have, you will find these skills invaluable.

I've also used these skills in my current profession as a researcher. Beall Research is a strategic market research firm that conducts studies for Fortune 500 companies. We often interview consumers to understand their needs, desires, and reactions. Being able to read their body language is tremendously useful and has allowed us to understand what really matters to them. The ability to see beyond just what they say had led to insights that have been valuable to our customers.

Whatever you use this learning for, you'll find it invaluable. Welcome to the world of PERCEIVE!

ACKNOWLEDGMENTS

There are two people in my life who have had a huge influence on my ability and interest in reading nonverbal communications. The first person is my mother, Barbara Beall. She taught me at an early age to pay more attention to what people do than to what they say. She showed me that people's behavior is often more revealing than anything they can tell you about themselves. I discovered that this lesson is invaluable in assessing people and situations. To this day, I advise customers to spend more time watching what people do and less time listening to what they say. The other person who had a major influence on me was Florence "Lindy" Geis, my undergraduate adviser at the University of Delaware. Lindy designed some ingenious experiments that showed how people often have nonverbal responses to female leaders that are almost imperceptible and that undermine these leaders. Lindy was the first person to encourage me in my early interest in nonverbal communication and to show me how important it is in everyday interactions.

I would like to thank numerous people who contributed to the content of this book. I owe a debt of gratitude to the field of psychology and to the many researchers who published work that I used to create PERCEIVE. The thinking of this book was shaped by my training as a social psychological researcher, and I draw heavily on this background. My graduate adviser, Bob Sternberg, has played an important role in my professional life and continues to encourage me in my various pursuits. Although other advisers discouraged their students from entering the "real world," he completely encouraged my endeavors and supported the application of psychological research findings to the business world.

I would also like to thank the many people who have encouraged me in the development and dissemination of PERCEIVE. Numerous people have engaged my services as a speaker for their organizations. There are far too many people to name, but they have had a lasting influence on this work.

CHAPTER 1: WHAT BODY LANGUAGE REVEALS AND WHY

This impossibility of not communicating is extremely
important to understand because it means that each of us is a
kind of transmitter that cannot be shut off. No matter what we
do, we give off information about ourselves.
—Adler & Proctor[1]

The quote above captures the essence of nonverbal communication. It's a part of our communication that can be read at any time, and unlike speech, you can't just turn it off. You can choose not to speak, but you can never be silent nonverbally. Regardless of whether you're sitting reading a book or talking with another person, you're constantly saying something with your body. This type of communication can provide tremendous insight into what people think and feel—almost as if they are broadcasting their thoughts and feelings to us. But why is that so? Why does nonverbal communication reveal so much?

Why Nonverbal Communication Reveals So Much

Nonverbal communication is highly revealing because there is so much of it and because people don't control it well. Approximately 60–93 percent of communication is nonverbal in nature.[2] That is a tremendous amount of communication that's available to read. Much of this communication is something that people are either unaware of or unable to control effectively.[3] We control our speech relatively well when it comes to saying the right things for the right occasion. But although our words may be the right ones, our bodies can betray us. A good example of this situation occurred with a colleague of mine. She did a favor for me while I was on a business trip. I thought it would be a nice gesture to buy her a gift, and I gave her a beautiful scarf upon my return. She opened the present and said, "Thank you, I love it." However, her eyes told me a different story. She didn't look at the scarf for very long and quickly put it on the table. As you will learn in a future chapter, people look longer at things they like. Her eyes told me that she didn't like the scarf. She admitted to me later that it wasn't something that fit her style.

Part of the reason we're unable to control our nonverbal communication is that it occurs across so many parts of the body, which are difficult to manage simultaneously. Unlike words, which provide information via their content and some of the qualities of the voice (such as the tone and the speed of utterance), nonverbal communication involves the entire body—one's face, eyes, body posture, hand movements, body orientation, proximity, and so on. That's a lot to manage at one time. It's not surprising that people aren't able to fake certain things nonverbally. Just watching what one says can be demanding, let alone trying to control one's facial expressions, posture, gestures, and everything else. Because there are so many areas to control, feelings will leak out in one or more parts of the body. In fact, that's what makes nonverbal communication so daunting—that there is so much of it to attend to when it comes to reading people. However, it's worth learning to read it because it reveals so many things. Below are some of the things that people reveal with their body language.

Nonverbal Communication Reveals Interest and Engagement

One of the best ways to tell if someone is interested and engaged with you is to look at her nonverbal behavior. As you'll learn in future chapters, specific nonverbal behaviors indicate whether a person is interested in what you're saying. When I give presentations, I always watch the body language of the attendees because their behaviors subtly tell me if they're engaged with the topic. Interest and engagement are also the first stages in any kind of professional relationship. If your boss, colleagues, or customers are not interested in what you have to say, it's important to know. And if you're in sales, the first step toward establishing a relationship with customers involves getting their interest.

Once you've read whether the person is interested in you and your topic, you have the chance to extend that relationship. If the person isn't interested, the sooner you identify that issue, the greater the chance you have to salvage the situation. I've seen countless examples of people just droning on while a client is showing clear signs of disinterest. Unfortunately, the person is oblivious to this fact and continues to bore his customer. Every minute that he doesn't read the situation leads to irritation and assures that he won't create a good relationship with this person.

Nonverbal Communication Reveals Liking and Dislike

We also reveal whom we like and dislike by what we do nonverbally. Generally we don't express our dislike for others openly. But we do experience a multitude of feelings about the people with whom we work. At one point or another we've all strongly disliked a boss, colleague, or client. Although professional etiquette doesn't allow us to express these feelings, we reveal them by how much we look at a person, how closely we stand or sit near him, and what expressions appear on our faces. Nonverbal behaviors are a rich source of information about feelings for others.

Feelings of liking and dislike in professional situations are an important source of information that can be used to advantage. If you determine that a customer doesn't like you, you may not want to waste your time with that person. There may be nothing that you can say to change the fact that you look like a hated ex-spouse. Let a colleague handle that person. And if you're in a job where your manager or major colleagues don't like you, it might not be the best place for you to work. Or it may provide you with an opportunity to win them over or make changes to your professional behavior.

Nonverbal Communications Reveal Emotions

Human beings are by nature emotional creatures. We experience emotions on a regular basis, but we generally don't express them in ways that are obvious. In the past hour, I've experienced several emotions. I've thought about my plans for the weekend, considered how to deal with a difficult person, and thought about someone who said something rude to me. I've experienced happiness, frustration, and anger. However, my colleagues didn't see anything visible to indicate these states. Although my emotions may not have been displayed strongly on my face, they would have been evident to someone who was looking closely at the subtle indications of my feelings.

Because professional situations don't encourage displays of strong emotions, we learn how to hide them. But we're never entirely successful. Emotions can leak out on our faces through microexpressions and subtle expressions. Emotions also leak out through our eye behavior, posture, orientation, gestures, and in other ways. Although we tend to look at people's faces to find their feelings, emotional expression often occurs all over the body, and you can spot it if you know where to look.

Clearly, knowing how someone else is feeling can be tremendously useful when dealing with others. Because I'm adept at reading others, I've been sensitive to others' feelings when they revealed them through their body language. I've observed that something is painful or something is important completely through their nonverbal communication. Because I can connect with these individuals emotionally, we have a much greater bond as a result. And that's part of establishing successful relationships.

Nonverbal Communication Reveals the Nature of a Relationship

Body language also reveals the kinds of relationships that people have with those around them. Because people show how they feel about others, it becomes clear which relationships are strong. Nonverbal communication also reveals who has higher status, who is respected, and who the leaders are in a group. You can tell whether someone is talking to their manager or to a friend just by observing how they stand relative to each other, what types of expressions they show, how closely or far apart they stand, and who initiates the beginning and end of the conversation. You can often tell these things without being able to hear what's said.

Knowing the types of relationships people have with one another can help one manage new situations. In some client situations, I've assessed the leadership team and been able to spot people who like and dislike each other, and to see the alliances within a group. Knowing which people are allied has been very useful in terms of determining why certain decisions get made and why some people exercise (or don't exercise) power in certain situations.

Nonverbal Communication Reveals What People Wish to Conceal

Most of us don't wish to reveal our thoughts and feelings to everyone all the time. In fact, we live in a culture that doesn't encourage tremendous emotional displays, particularly in the workplace. We don't typically cry at our desks at work, skip down the halls in happiness, or punch colleagues who frustrate us. The rules of expression in a society are called cultural display rules, and they vary depending on the emotion, the person expressing it, and the situation.[4] Because we don't always feel internally what the cultural display rules dictate, our nonverbal behavior can reveal feelings that we wish to conceal. We may not actually be sad at a funeral or happy at a wedding. And although we're expected to say certain things or act in a specific way, our nonverbal behavior can reveal what we really feel.

Nonverbal communication is also one of the best sources for telling that someone is lying. One of the classic studies in this area videotaped people telling truths and lies. The videotapes were then shown to other groups of people to see if they could discern when someone was lying. Each group looked or listened for a specific thing. One group looked only at people's faces, one group looked only at their bodies, one group only listened to their speech, and the last group just read what each person had said. Those who looked at only the person's body were the most accurate at determining when the individual was lying. Another way to tell if someone is lying is to look at the entire body including the face. If there are inconsistencies in what is shown on the face and what is displayed elsewhere, it is likely that the person is being deceitful.

Nonverbal Communication Reveals Feelings We Don't Admit Even to Ourselves

One interesting thing about human beings is that sometimes we don't even know what we feel. One aspect of emotional intelligence involves being able to read our own emotions, and sometimes we aren't very adept at that. We may have an uneasy, anxious feeling and don't know why. Reading another person's nonverbal communication, particularly in reaction to different people and situations, can give us insight into people—sometimes more than they have about themselves. This situation happened for me when I was looking to purchase my first condominium. I told the real estate agent that I was looking for a two-bedroom, two-bathroom apartment. She showed me more than fifty different condominiums—all two-bedroom, two-bathroom apartments. I didn't like any of them. Finally after a year of looking, she showed me a one-bedroom, one-bathroom apartment with a view of the city. I was sold. It turns out that I wasn't looking for a two-bedroom, two-bathroom apartment at all. I was looking for a view! If she had been reading my nonverbal communication, she would have realized what really mattered to me. The first thing that I did whenever I walked into a condominium was go straight to the window and look at the view. My looks of displeasure after seeing so many bad vistas should have told her everything. Reading another person's nonverbal communication allows us to obtain insight into the human heart and allows us to travel to places that words will never take us.

A System for Interpreting Nonverbal Communication (PERCEIVE)

Have you ever had a feeling that someone didn't like you but you weren't sure how you knew that? Have you ever thought that someone was lying to you but you weren't sure what gave you that impression? Have you ever had a gut feeling about someone and you didn't know why? In each of these situations, you were probably reading the person's body language and your mind was telling you something was awry. You may have regarded this feeling as an *instinct* because you didn't have a way of interpreting what you were seeing nonverbally. This experience happens because we aren't taught how to read others' body language. Our teachers and parents didn't teach us how to read others when we were learning other basic skills. As a result, we just have a *feeling* that something is going on but no systematic way to understand it.

The objective of this book is to give you a method for reading nonverbal communication so you can begin to interpret the hidden communications around you that are often difficult to understand.

The method that I will share is called PERCEIVE. It's one way of *perceiving* other people that I've found useful as a way to interpret the many aspects of nonverbal communication. It's also easy to remember. Each letter of PERCEIVE refers to a major piece of body language. "P" stands for Proximity, "E" is for Expressions, "R" is for Relative orientation, "C" is for Contact (physical touching), "E" is for Eyes, "I" is for Individual gestures, "V" is for Voice, and "E" stands for Existence of adaptors, which are those small fidgety behaviors that can speak volumes.

You may be wondering why nonverbal communication has to be so complicated. Why can't you just learn about one area and use that to read a person? The short answer is that nonverbal behavior occurs across one's entire body and you have to read it *all* to tell you the whole story. Just learning one thing can lead to spurious conclusions about another person. For example, one of the major myths is that when a person crosses her arms, it means that she's closed off and disinterested. There's no evidence that crossing one's arms is indicative of that at all. And yet, people consistently tell me that crossing one's arms reveals inner thoughts. You can see what crossed arms reveal when you look at the person's entire body. If the rest of her body language says she's disinterested in the conversation, then she's closed herself off. However, if her arms are crossed and she's leaning forward and showing attentive eye behavior, then her crossed arms are probably because she's cold or she feels more comfortable that way. Only when you read the entire person do you get the whole story. That's the beauty of nonverbal communication—it gives you multiple places to read.

You may be wondering how PERCEIVE was developed and the basis for it. Why not OBSERVE or SEE or ASPARAGUS? PERCEIVE was born after an exhaustive review of the major studies conducted by academic researchers in the fields of psychology, anthropology, and communication. The research literature revealed some basic findings about nonverbal communication that have been replicated in numerous studies. Any finding that was not replicated across several studies isn't included. PERCEIVE is based on this body of research, and it summarizes all the major areas of nonverbal communication: the face, body, voice (such as tone and cadence), and hands. As an aside, this research was mostly conducted in English-speaking countries such as the United States, Canada, and Australia. And I do point out areas where cultural differences occur. The basic principles of what I will discuss, however, apply to most societies.

How This Book Is Organized

I discuss each of the aspects of PERCEIVE in the following chapters. Each chapter provides a different insight into nonverbal communication, and I highlight real examples of how you can read each part of body language and use it to your advantage.

- Chapter 2 is about proximity and relative orientation, which are the foundation for all body language.
- Chapter 3 is about expressions that appear on the face. Although most people think they can read basic expressions, I'll show you how

complicated facial expression can be and how to read the most subtle ones.

- Chapter 4 is about contact (physical contact), which is revealing of some of the stronger feelings we have about people.
- Chapter 5 is about the eyes, and you will learn how the eyes reveal volumes about how we feel about ourselves and others.
- Chapter 6 is about gestures, which reveal a great deal about the images in people's minds and how they see the world.
- Chapter 7 is about the voice and the paralinguistic qualities of speech such as tone and rapidity, which reveal many things about what a speaker is feeling.
- Chapter 8 is about adaptors, which are those small fidgety behaviors that can reveal periods of stress or boredom.
- Chapter 9 is about electronic communications, which are a frequent way we communicate.
- Chapter 10 is about putting all the learning together and using it to read an entire person.

In the beginning of the following chapters, there is a section called "Some Basic Ideas." This information is meant to provide some generalities about each part of PERCEIVE. At the end of every chapter (except chapter 9), there is a section titled "Things to Think About," which provides some additional things to consider when observing that aspect of body language. This section is followed by "The Least You Need to Know," which summarizes the major lessons from the chapter. The last part of the chapter is called "Improving your Ability to Read [each area]." This section provides some exercises that you can use to become proficient in reading and interpreting each area of PERCEIVE.

How to Use This Book

There is no question that nonverbal behavior is complicated. However, with PERCEIVE, it will be simplified for you. Each chapter covers a major area of the system and some ways that you can use this knowledge. The goal of this book is to help you observe nonverbal behavior of customers and colleagues, and to use PERCEIVE to make some educated assessments of those around you and react accordingly.

Because it takes time to master reading nonverbal behavior, I recommend that you read each chapter and then spend some time observing that specific area to become adept at reading people. At the end of each chapter there's a section on how to improve your ability to read each particular area. Do the exercises, because they will help you observe each aspect and they will be very useful in revealing things about the people around you. Try to master each area of nonverbal communication before going on to the next chapter. If you try to learn all the nonverbal areas at once, it may feel overwhelming and could be confusing. By mastering one area at a time, reading all nonverbal communication will eventually come easily to you.

One of the best ways to increase your abilities in this arena is to watch movies or television with the volume turned all the way down. Watch a program that you're familiar with and have seen several times. What can you tell about the people from their facial expressions? What other nonverbal behaviors tell you things about their current situation? Try to guess what's going on based just on observing the people without any sound. Try to see which nonverbal behaviors help you the most in understanding the current thoughts and feelings of each character. Watch it for five to ten minutes and then turn up the volume. What did you learn about each person just based on the nonverbal behavior? You will be amazed at how much you can pick up.

The Least You Need to Know

- Nonverbal behavior reveals so much because there is a great deal of it and people don't control it well.
- Nonverbal communication reveals:
  - interest and engagement with another person;
  - our feelings of like or dislike for someone;
  - emotional experiences;
  - the nature of a relationship between two people;
  - lying and things we wish to conceal;
  - feelings we don't admit even to ourselves.
- PERCEIVE is a way to interpret nonverbal communication.
- It is based on a large body of research conducted by researchers in the fields of psychology, anthropology, and communication.

References

1. Adler, R., B. & Proctor, R. F. (2017). *Looking out looking in.* Boston, Massachusetts: Cengage Learning

2. Hickson, M., Stacks, D. W., & Moore, N. (2004). *Nonverbal communication: Studies and applications.* Los Angeles: Roxbury.

3. Ekman, P., & Friesen, W. V. (1968). Nonverbal behavior in psychotherapy research. *Psychotherapy, 3,* 88–106.

4. Matsumoto, D. (2006). Culture and nonverbal behavior. In V. Manusov & M. Patterson (Eds.), *The Sage handbook of nonverbal communication.* Thousand Oaks, CA: Sage Publications.

CHAPTER 2: PROXIMITY AND RELATIVE ORIENTATION

Proximity and relative orientation are the foundation of all nonverbal communication. All of the remaining body language occurs within the context of these two things. Proximity is the closeness between two people. Relative orientation is the degree to which you directly or indirectly face another person. One's proximity and relative orientation are the major ways that we interact with another person and reveal a great deal about our liking for others.

Some Basic Ideas:

Generally speaking, people tend to sit or stand more closely to those they like, those they're more interested in, and those people they want to get to know.

People also tend to face more directly those they like, those they want to get to know, and those they're more interested in.

Proximity Reveals Liking and Involvement

Proximity is the first indication of our involvement and interest in another person. We approach those whom we know and like more closely than we approach strangers.[1,2] Thus, we will sit and stand nearer our close friends than our acquaintances. And when we expect to have a good interaction with someone, we typically get closer to them. We also tend to approach others who are physically attractive more closely than those who aren't.[3] Interestingly, we give much more space to people who have stigmas—either a physical stigma such as being scarred or handicapped, or a social stigma such as being a convict.[4,5,6] Thus, we tend to get near those whom we like and those whom we expect to like, even if we don't actually know them.

You can see this effect in office seating. If you have an office with a guest chair, watch how closely the next person puts the guest chair in relation to you. Some people will pull their chair close to you as soon as they sit down. Others will move their chair away if they feel the interaction distance is too close. People often move a chair very subtly, so you have to watch closely. The amount of proximity reveals what they feel about you and what they expect from the interaction. If they don't expect to have a good interaction, they will sit farther away. Also notice where a person sits in his chair. Some people will sit all the way forward in a chair, whereas others will sit all the way back against the chair. The movement closer to you reveals that they like you and are engaged in the meeting. Sometimes you will see changes in proximity during the course of a meeting. Watch what happens when you discuss something that the person wants to discuss; you may see them sit forward or lean toward you. You can also see this behavior at meetings that occur at a table. You can tell who likes whom by seeing who sits together. You can also gauge interest in different topics. When people are interested in certain ones, they tend to sit closer to the table.

Proximity Reveals Type of Relationship

Because one's proximity indicates interest and involvement with another person, the closer people tend to stand or sit relative to one another, the closer the relationship. We keep different distances around us depending on the type of relationship we have with a person.[7] In North America, the *intimate distance* is reserved for those with whom we have the closest relationships: our romantic partners, family members, and very close friends. It extends to eighteen inches around us. *Personal distance* extends from one and a half to four feet away and is used with friends and acquaintances. *Social distance* is between four and eight feet away from the body and is typically used for professional interactions—the ones we have with salespeople, teachers, consultants, and other businesspeople. The last zone is called *public distance* and is eight feet away or more from the body. This is the distance that we would like strangers to stand from us when we take a public bus or subway. See the photos for examples of the different interpersonal-distance zones.

Intimate Distance

Personal Distance

Social Distance

Public Distance

Knowing the different interpersonal distances for each type of relationship helps you understand the nature of the relationships you observe around you, as well as the kinds of relationships that you have with your colleagues and customers. One of the most important ways you can use this information is to understand when you have transcended certain categories such as *vendor* or *work associate*. For example, when you first begin working with someone, it's normal for the two of you to interact in the social-distance space. However, if the relationship progresses to a high level of trust and collegiality, you may begin to interact in the personal-distance space. And if you become an important, trusted person, you may progress to the intimate distance. I always watch the amount of space my clients use with me because that tells me how they feel about me. If they put me in the personal or intimate space, I can see that I'm more than just a vendor and have become a trusted adviser to them.

Personality, Gender and Cultural Differences in Proximity

Proximity can also reveal a great deal about another individual's personality. Personality traits such as introversion and extroversion influence the amount of distance that people keep between themselves and others.[8] Introverted people, as the term implies, tend to be inward turned and engage with others less than extroverts. They don't dislike social interactions, but they can find them fatiguing and tend to have larger interpersonal distances. In contrast, extroverted folks tend to become energized by other people and tend to keep smaller distances between themselves and others. Extroverts love interacting with other people, and their interpersonal distances show that. If you observe a client or colleague regularly sitting farther away from you and other people, this individual may be an introvert. If you observe another person regularly sitting and standing closely to you and others, then you're probably dealing with an extrovert.

Gender also influences proximity to others.[9] Men tend to use larger interpersonal distances than women. Women tend to approach others more closely and to be approached more closely than men.[10] As a result, the largest distances occur between two men and the smallest distances occur between two women. Proximity between men and women falls somewhere between these two interpersonal distances.[11,12] The interesting thing is that men and women maintain these proximities in virtual environments. Researchers have studied interactions in Second Life, which is a virtual world where people interact through avatars (digital representations of themselves). Men keep a larger distance when interacting with other men than they do in male-female interactions.[13] It's important to keep these gender differences in mind when observing men and women. If you see two men interacting fairly far apart, you want to keep in mind that men tend to stand farther apart from one another, and their distance is caused in part by their gender and the type of relationship they have with each other.

Culture also influences the distance between people. For example, Americans tend to work and conduct business within a four-foot range from one another. However, people from Middle Eastern cultures tend to stand much closer[14]. This difference in expected proximity can lead to perceptions that are inaccurate. As a result of these spatial differences, Arabs may regard US people as condescending and aloof whereas North Americans may regard Middle Easterners as arrogant and overbearing[15].

Are You in the Right Space?

One thing to keep in mind is that you interact with people at certain distances also. You may feel strongly about someone so you interact with them in your personal space. How do you know if that's the right space from their point of view? There isn't anything quite like the feeling you get when someone stands or sits too closely. It's uncomfortable. How do you know if *you* have invaded someone's space and the person doesn't like it? Generally people will respond with subtle behaviors that can be almost imperceptible.[16,17,18] When a person's space is violated, she will move slightly backward—by moving either her whole body backward or just her neck and head. The person may also turn her body slightly to the side to compensate for the invasion. Or there can be a loss of eye contact and a pause in the conversation.

Interestingly, there are some space invasions that people will tolerate. People who are higher in status or *high in reward value* have a greater ability to invade the spaces of others.[19] Those who are high in reward value tend to be physically attractive people, well-dressed individuals, work superiors, or people who have any major positive quality. So, if you see your colleague Tom getting his space invaded by another person at a party, the space invader is probably tolerated if he or she offers something positive to Tom. If the space invader is Tom's supervisor or an attractive woman he's wanted to meet, Tom may tolerate the space invasion more politely and for longer than if it's a subordinate or the annoying guy from the copy-machine room. In general, people who are higher in status tend to have larger person spaces and greater privacy afforded to them as a result of their position[20].

Relative Orientation Reveals Interest and Involvement

Relative orientation describes how people are positioned relative to one another. Similar to proximity, we tend to directly face those whom we like and with whom we have the greatest involvement. As a professional speaker I've noticed that people will slightly change their body orientation as I pace the floor. I've also noticed that if people begin to be disinterested, they will stop orienting toward me. That's the case for all interactions. In fact, a sign that one is ending a conversation is the half turn that we tend to do when we are ready to exit an interaction. See the next photo, which shows this change in orientation that signals the end of the conversation.

Ending a Conversation

One can use changes in orientation to great advantage in the workplace. If you see that a person is becoming disinterested in a conversation, you can let it take its course or you can intervene. One of the most useful techniques for reengaging a person who has become disinterested is to ask him a question. I often do this if clients start to orient away from me when I'm speaking. I'll ask them about their current needs or get a reaction to what I've been saying. Subtle changes in orientation can be very useful if you're paying attention, because you can use them to ensure that you never overstay your welcome in a conversation.

Relative Orientation Reveals Power, Competition, and Cooperation

In group settings, relative orientation can provide information about power and personality. People who are leaders of a group tend to occupy the positions at the end of a rectangular table. However, what's interesting is that people believe a person who sits at the end of a table is a leader even if those seats are assigned randomly. Part of the reason people at the end of the table tend to be chosen as the leader is that this position is a visually central one, which means that these positions receive more undivided gaze than other positions at the table. Those who are in visually central positions tend to have more influence on a group because this central position tends to engender more talking than other positions. At a rectangular table, the dominant seating positions are spaces one, three, and five, as shown below.[21] Individuals who choose to sit in these seats tend to talk more and to be dominant personalities. Those who choose to sit in positions two and four tend to be less dominant and report that they want to stay verbally out of a discussion.

1

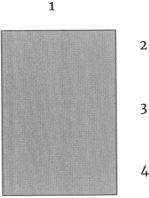

2

3

4

5

Relative orientation can also reveal information about whether people are competing or cooperating with one another. In a classic study, researchers asked participants where they would like to sit at a rectangular table for specific situations: 1) conversing about a topic, 2) cooperating—studying together for the same exam, and 3) competing—trying to beat one another at a competitive task. As shown in the next figure, when people are conversing or cooperating, they say they're likely to sit near one another—either side by side, alongside the corner of a table, or directly across when conversing. However, when they're competing, they favor the ends of the table, sitting directly across from one another with as much space as possible between them.[22]

Favored Seating Positions

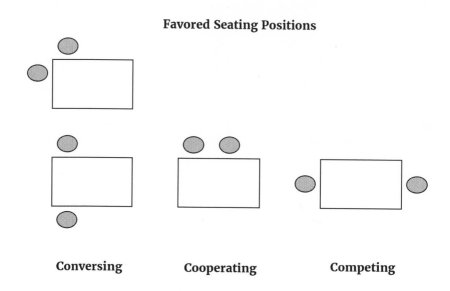

Conversing   **Cooperating**   **Competing**

Knowing this information about relative orientation helps you understand the dynamics of a group. Watch where people sit in meetings, because seating can reveal the participants' intentions and personality attributes. Watch who sits in the most visually central positions and who doesn't. Those who sit in these positions are most likely to be the dominant personalities and are likely to talk the most. Also watch where people sit when it's just you and another person. Given that people tend to sit catty-corner from one another when cooperating, those who sit directly across from you (particularly when this distance is farther away than a catty-corner seat) may be less interested in cooperating. In client situations, I always consider it a bad sign when a new client sits directly across from me because it suggests that it's not a partnership but more of an evaluation right from the beginning. One thing you can do is try to take the corner seat after someone sits down to handle the proximity and orientation right from the beginning. Of course, sometimes seating is dictated by where chairs are and you can sit only in a specific configuration because of the constraints of a room.

It's also useful to watch how proximities and orientations change during a meeting. The person that people want to sit closest to are typically the ones with the highest status or the ones perceived as having the most interesting or useful things to say. If everyone is oriented directly toward Graham right from the beginning of the meeting, that tells you about Graham's status in that organization. If people lean forward when Dylan talks, that reveals that they're interested in what he's saying. If people don't turn toward Dylan or lean forward when he talks, that's an indication that the group isn't particularly interested in him or what he's saying.

Gender Differences in Relative Orientation

Men and women differ in how directly they tend to orient toward other people. Women tend to orient more directly toward others than men.[23] Two men will have the least direct orientation and may even sit at angles to each other. Two women will sit or stand face-to-face and will often have the most direct orientations. Men and women interacting together should fall between these two extremes on the continuum of body orientation. It's important to keep these gender norms in mind when evaluating colleagues. If Katherine isn't oriented directly toward you, that says more than if Tom doesn't orient directly toward you, given the gender norms for body orientation.

Some Things to Think About

You will want to keep several general things in mind when observing the proximity and orientation of others:

- Observe the person's typical proximity and orientation and her deviations from them. If Tammy is typically a "close talker" and she interacts with you at a greater distance, that is a sign that she is less involved, less interested, or likes you less than she likes other people.
- Observe the proximity and orientation that most people have in that situation and any deviations from it. People attending a friendly luncheon will tend to have closer proximities and more direct orientations than those at a formal meeting. However, if Gary interacts with you more closely at a formal meeting than is the norm, he probably likes you.

The Least You Need to Know

- We stand and sit closer to those we like, those we're interested in, and those we expect to like.
- The closer we interact with people physically, the closer our relationship tends to be with them.
- You can tell if you've invaded someone's space if she moves very subtly backward, turns her body slightly, loses eye contact, or pauses in the conversation.
- Introverts tend to keep larger interpersonal distances than extroverts.
- Men tend to keep larger interpersonal distances than women.
- We tend to orient more directly toward those we like, those we expect to like, and those we're interested in knowing.
- Orientations toward people in a group reveal status and personality attributes. Dominant personalities tend to take the seating positions in a group that are visually central.
- Relative orientation also reveals competition and cooperation. Those who are competing tend to sit across from one another and tend to sit farther apart. Those who are cooperating tend to sit next to or closely across from one another.
- Men tend to have less direct orientations with others, particularly with other men. Women tend to have more direct orientations when interacting with others.

Improving Your Ability to Read Proximity and Relative Orientation

Below are some ways to improve your ability to read proximity and orientation.

- Notice the proximities of people who are in different relationships: Look at how closely two romantic partners interact, two friends, and two work colleagues who are not close friends. Now look at the proximities of people you don't know and try to guess the nature of their relationships.
- Notice the orientations that people have toward one another while they're conversing. Can you tell when the interaction is almost over by a change in the proximity or orientation?
- Notice whom people are oriented toward in a meeting. Where are their bodies facing? Are they oriented toward the most powerful or influential

person in the room? Do they turn their bodies toward that person when he or she speaks? What does orientation tell you about influence in a group?

- Notice other orientation and proximity behavior during meetings. Do specific people turn and lean toward others they like when that person is speaking? Do some people orient toward some individuals but not toward others when they are speaking? What does orientation tell you about who likes whom in a group?
- Notice where people sit in a meeting. Can you tell who is competing and who is cooperating with whom by where they sit?

References

1. Edwards, D. J. A. (1972). Approaching the unfamiliar: A study of human interaction distances. *Journal of Behavioral Science, 1,* 249–250.
2. Little, K. B. (1965). Personal space. *Journal of Experimental Social Psychology, 1,* 237–247.
3. Allgeir, A. R., & Byrne, D. (1973). Attraction toward the opposite sex as a determinant of physical proximity. *Journal of Social Psychology, 90,* 213–219.
4. Barrios, B. A., Corbitt, L. C., Estes, J. P., & Topping, J. S. (1976). Effect of a social stigma on interpersonal distance. *Psychological Record, 26,* 343–348.
5. Mallenby, T. W. (1974). Personal space—direct measurement techniques with hard of hearing students. *Environment and Behavior, 6,* 117–121.
6. Worthington, M. E. (1974). Personal space as a function of the stigma effect. *Environment and Behavior, 6,* 289–294.
7. Remland M. S. (2000). *Nonverbal communication in everyday life.* Boston: Houghton Mifflin.
8. Richmond, V. P., & McCroskey, J. C. (2000). *Nonverbal behavior in interpersonal relations.* Needham Heights, MA: Allyn & Bacon.
9. Richmond, V. P., & McCroskey, J. C. (2000). *Nonverbal behavior in interpersonal relations.* Needham Heights, MA: Allyn & Bacon.
10. Hall. J. A. (1984). *Nonverbal sex differences: Accuracy of communication and expressive style.* Baltimore: Johns Hopkins University Press.
11. Adler, L., & Iverson, M. (1974). Interpersonal distance as a function of task difficulty, praise, status orientation and sex of partner. *Perceptual & Motor Skills, 39,* 623–692.

12. Aiello, J. (1977). A further look at equilibrium theory. Visual interaction as a function of interpersonal distance. *Environmental Psychology & Nonverbal Behavior, 1*, 122–140.

13. Yee, N., Balenson, J. N., Urbanek, M., Chang, F., & Merget, D. (2006). The unbearable likeness of being digital. The persistence of nonverbal social norms in online virtual environments. In L. K. Guerrero & M. L. Hecht (Eds.), *The nonverbal communication reader*. Long Grove, IL: Waveland Press.

14. Feghali, E. K. (1997). Arab cultural communication patterns. *International Journal of Intercultural Relations, 21*, 345-378.

15. Watson, O. M., (1970). *Proxemic behavior: A cross-cultural study.* The Hague: Mouton.

16. Burgoon, J. K., & Aho, L. (1982). Three field experiments on the effects of violations of conversational distance. *Communication Monographs, 49,* 70–88

17. Burgoon, J. K., & Jones, S. B. (1976). Toward a theory of personal space expectations and their violations. *Human Communication Research, 2,* 131–146

18. Burgoon, J. K., & Walther, J. B. (1990). Nonverbal expectancies and the evaluative consequences of violations. *Human Communication Research, 17,* 232–265.

19. Hickson, M., Stacks, D. W., & Moore, N. (2004). *Nonverbal communication: Studies and applications.* Los Angeles: Roxbury.

20. Brown, G., Lawrence, T. B., & Robinson, S. L. (2005). Territoriality in organizations. *Academy of Management Review, 30,* 577-594.

21. Hare, A., & Bales, R. (1963). Seating position and small group interaction. *Sociometry, 26,* 480–486.

22. Knapp, M. L., & Hall, J. H. (2002). *Nonverbal communication in human interaction.* Belmont, CA: Thomson Learning.

23. Hall. J. A. (1984). *Nonverbal sex differences: Accuracy of communication and expressive style.* Baltimore: Johns Hopkins University Press.

CHAPTER 3: EXPRESSIONS

Some Basic Ideas:

There are seven basic emotional expressions that are recognized by people across cultures: happiness, sadness, anger, surprise, fear, disgust, and contempt.

People tend to display milder versions of their feelings in the workplace, so internal feelings may be detected only through microexpressions and partial expressions.

Colleagues may convey expressions they don't feel in order to create certain interactions. False expressions have certain features that one can use to detect them.

Men and women are expected to display different emotional expressions in professional settings; women are expected to display happy expressions more than men, whereas men are expected to display more angry expressions than women.

It's amazing that in our multicultural world where people can dress, act, and think quite differently, some things are the same for all human beings. One of these things is facial expressions. There are seven universal facial expressions that are expressed and understood by humans all over the world: happiness, sadness, anger, disgust, fear, surprise, and contempt.[1] Emotional expressions certainly give us a universal language we can all use to communicate. We may not understand another person's verbal language, but we can understand her nonverbal one.

Interestingly, these expressions may be universal because they're the basic expressions upon which all other expressions are built. Our expressions are complicated because we sometimes show more than one at a time. For example, a woman who walks into a surprise party will probably express both surprise and happiness. Upon learning that a colleague has been dishonest, I express both sadness and anger. The many different variations of facial expressions are due to the mixture of these basic expressions.

In general people in the workplace don't show these expressions fully unless it's appropriate to do so. However, there is no doubt that human beings are highly emotional creatures and that we experience emotions fairly frequently. At many times during the day you will experience a variety of feelings—from happiness about some positive feedback you've just received to frustration with difficult customers or colleagues. And just because we don't show our feelings in an obvious way doesn't mean that we don't express them subtly. Evidence suggests that we tend to display muted and brief versions of many of the emotions we experience. Because these seven expressions are the major ones, we will explore how to spot each one. We will describe and show examples of the overt ones because the less overt versions have the same attributes.

How to Identify Happiness

The words *happy* and *happiness* are used in a few different ways. We often use them to refer to an enduring emotional state of self-fulfillment such as "He's a happy person" or "She's had a very happy life." We also use these terms to describe our reaction to pleasurable events such as when we say that certain events or experiences make us happy. The smile is the enduring expression of happiness. People experience many enjoyable emotions such as amusement, contentment, excitement, relief, wonderment, ecstasy, pride in oneself, pride in one's children, and gratitude.[2] Smiles can be associated with each one of these enjoyable emotions.

The smile is one of the most and one of the least effective ways of identifying these emotions. One of the reasons it's ineffective is because people often fake it. In the case where a client gave me a gift that I didn't care for, I smiled when I thanked her. My smile was not a good indication of how I really felt. Or was it? It turns out that the smile can be an extremely reliable way to discern what a person is feeling if you look closely at it.

There are two major types of smiles; one is false and the other is real. The real smile is called the Duchenne smile, named after a French scientist who discovered the difference between the two types of smiles. The real smile differs from a false smile in terms of whether the muscles around the eyes are activated or not. As you can see from the following pictures, people who are truly enjoying something smile with both their eyes and their mouth. The difference between the two expressions is clearly captured in the photo below, which is the real smile. As you can see, the eyes are narrower, the eyebrows are pulled down lower, and the cheeks are pulled up slightly more. The next photo is of a false smile. This smile uses the eyes less than the real one. Most photographs that we see in magazines show false smiles. And typically the photos we like of ourselves are false smiles because they don't show our eye wrinkles as much.

Real Smile

False Smile

Smiles can be very revealing. In one study, psychologists discovered that happily married couples who met at the end of the day used real smiles, whereas unhappily married couples tended to use false smiles.[3] Other studies have shown that people who tend to use a real smile more often report greater happiness overall. Interestingly, when people use the real smile, the eye muscles stimulate regions of the brain associated with enjoyment, whereas a false smile doesn't activate that region of the brain.[4] Thus, it's difficult to fake a real smile and difficult to portray a feeling one doesn't have. One can easily tell whether customers and colleagues are truly happy about something just by looking closely at the muscles around the eyes when they're smiling.

I once had a situation where a client asked me to work with a person in my field. When I met the person, she gushed with enthusiasm about how happy she was to meet me and how much she wanted to work with me on a specific project. However, I noticed that her smiles toward me were always false. I suspected that she was not as enthusiastic as she described and that she was putting on a show for the client's sake. I was right. She was fairly problematic to deal with and had little to no interest in partnering with me and had done so because the client had requested it. My initial meeting with her where she showed a false smile was a harbinger of things to come.

How to Identify Sadness

Sadness is an expression that also uses several parts of the face—namely the lips, chin, eyes, and eyebrows. As you can see in the next picture, sadness is distinguished by the inner corners of the eyebrows being slightly raised up. The eyelids are slightly closed and the lips are pulled down somewhat in almost a pout. The eyes may look like inverted almonds. Sadness is more easily identified from the eyes and eyelids than from the mouth. Sometimes a sad person will tend to look down or place her face in a downward position as if the weight of the world is upon her. One good indicator of sadness is that downward look of the eyes and head. People often become sad when they experience a loss or some type of defeat.

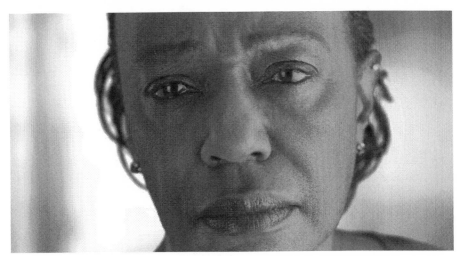

Sadness

How to Identify Anger

Anger is a relatively easy emotion to spot in others when it's fully expressed. As you can see in the next photo, anger is marked by knit eyebrows and lowered eyes. The eyebrows are drawn together, sometimes creating two lines between them. There is a great deal of action in the eyes and eyebrows when someone is angry. Anger is also distinguished by intense, glaring eyes. The mouth is generally tense and the lips are pressed together, or the mouth can be open and the teeth exposed when someone is angry. See the next photo for an example of anger.

One of the more interesting experiences I had with anger occurred with a client who worked for a large company and became angry in a large team meeting. He went on a tirade about the project we were supposed to be collaborating on with him. The interesting thing was that his facial expressions didn't reveal anger at all. He was putting on a show of anger for the people in the room. His goal was to intimidate us and to take over the project that we were doing. His display of anger had more to do with protecting his turf and showing his power than with his feelings. We decided not to partner with him as a result.

Anger

How to Identify Surprise

Surprise is the emotion that is the shortest in duration. It typically lasts only a few seconds at most. After the initial experience of surprise, we usually feel another emotion, so surprise will often turn into fear, happiness, anger, or some other feeling. The distinguishing characteristics of surprise are wide eyes, raised eyebrows, and often an open mouth with the upper and lower teeth slightly parted. The eyebrows tend to be curved and raised. Surprise tends to be accompanied by wrinkles on the forehead, which is the result of the eyebrows being raised.

Surprise is one of the most interesting things to watch in the corporate world. I notice who seems surprised when they hear news that a senior manager is leaving or that the company is restructuring. Those people who are truly surprised will show it with their eyes and their forehead. The best way to tell quickly is just to look at the forehead. If you don't see wrinkles, the person isn't surprised. See the next photo for an extreme example of surprise.

Surprise

How to Identify Fear

Fear is also an expression that is quick in duration. It can sometimes start out as surprise and then become full-blown fear. The expression of fear involves the eyebrows, which are raised and may be slightly pulled together. Often the upper eyelids are raised—the more they are raised, the more fearful the person is. There is also a glare in the eyes and a tension in the lips. Often the lips are pulled back and can sometimes reveal the teeth. True fear is a relatively unusual emotion to see in the workplace. It's more common to see signs of anxiety and worry than true fear. I discuss what behaviors are indicators of anxiety, stress, and boredom in chapter 8. See the next photo for an extreme example of fear.

Fear

How to Identify Disgust

This expression is often inadvertently shown in reaction to things that smell or taste bad. We don't control it easily, particularly in circumstances when we have a bodily reaction to something that's unpleasant. However, disgust is also expressed in response to ideas and people whom we dislike. It can be a somewhat subtle expression.

The hallmarks of disgust are the lowering of the eyebrows and a wrinkling of the nose along with a raised upper lip. Disgust tends to be expressed around the center of the face, particularly the nose. Watch closely how people react to others' ideas and sometimes you can see subtle signs of disgust by a wrinkling of the nose. See the following picture for an example of disgust.

Disgust

How to Identify Contempt

The last basic expression is contempt, which is similar to disgust in its negativity. However, we typically experience contempt in reaction to people rather than tastes and smells. Rotting, smelly garbage would cause us to experience disgust, not contempt. We would feel disgust upon discovering the garbage in the break room and contempt for the person who put it there. Contempt is the only expression that is asymmetrical and uses one side of the face more than the other. Contempt is typically shown by one corner of the mouth being tightened and raised slightly. Thus, if you see an asymmetrical expression, you're probably seeing contempt. Expressions of contempt occur fairly often in the workplace. They are usually momentary, fleeting expressions that are often expressed in reaction to people and ideas. See the next photo for an example.

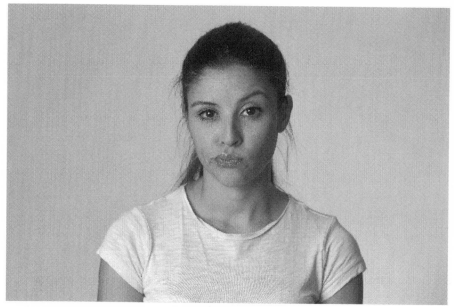

Contempt

The Value in Being Able to Spot Microexpressions

Many work environments require that we show less overt expressions than what we may feel. One isn't encouraged to show full-blown anger at a colleague who has not done his job, but some minor irritation may be acceptable in certain circumstances. As a result, we don't have the luxury of being able to spot the full-blown expressions that were depicted in the previous photographs. So how do you spot emotions that people are trying to hide? The answer lies in observing microexpressions.

Microexpressions are emotional expressions that occur for a very brief period that we cannot control. Researchers have discovered that when we experience an emotion, it triggers the muscles in the face.[5] Even when we suppress a full facial expression, we are able to suppress it only after it has started to show. The resulting expression occurs for about one-quarter of a second. That's generally not long enough for most people to notice it, but if you're very observant, you can see these microexpressions. If you've ever had the experience of thinking you saw an expression briefly on someone's face, it was probably a microexpression.

Because microexpressions are not controlled, they're a good indicator of when someone is telling a lie. Researchers have determined that individuals who are trained to spot microexpressions can accurately identify 80 percent of truths and lies on average.[6] Because microexpressions are such a good indication of deceit, several law enforcement agencies have received training on how to recognize them. The Department of Homeland Security invested more than $3.5 million in research in this topic,[7] and investigators such as Paul Ekman and Mark Frank have assisted in training employees of police agencies and institutions such as the Department of Homeland Security, the CIA, and the FBI on how to spot microexpressions.[8,9]

One doesn't have to become an airport screener to see the utility of this skill in workplace situations. An example of how this can be used occurred in an initial meeting I had with a potential client. A colleague and I were presenting our capabilities to a large pharmaceutical company in New York. As my colleague was speaking, the potential client showed a microexpression of contempt on his face. He began to pull his chair back from the table, which decreased his proximity to us. I realized that what my colleague was saying was not resonating and that he was beginning to disengage from us and from the presentation. I interrupted my colleague and said to the potential client, "Before we go any further, how well do these capabilities address your current needs?" The potential client replied that they didn't meet his needs and that he was looking for different services. We then spoke specifically to his needs and ended up winning business from that company. My quick response to his microexpression allowed us to address his objections before he became fully disengaged and decided he didn't want to work with us.

Further Emotion Spotting: Partial Expressions

The other fascinating aspect of facial expressions is that we sometimes suppress them on *only part* of our face. The resulting expression is a partial expression. For example, instead of seeing a microexpression of sadness you might see just the upper eyebrows being raised or a slight pout in the mouth. Partial expressions are sometimes indicative of the beginning of an emotional expression or of a very low-level emotional experience.[10] In either case, these expressions can be illuminating about professional interactions. Clearly seeing the initial signs of happiness or sadness can reveal that someone is starting to feel something or starting to suppress an emotional expression. On more than one occasion, I've seen a slight sign of anger or irritation between colleagues, which has spoken volumes about the underlying feelings between these two people. See examples of partial expressions in the next photos.

Partial expression of sadness

Partial expression of happiness

Overt Emotional Expressions Don't Always Reveal True Feelings

Because emotional expressions are also communication tools, we can also read them in terms of the expresser's motivations. You can think about them as a way to create a certain type of interaction and not necessarily a reflection of the person's feelings. For example, we may show sadness as a way of displaying pity for someone or we may show contempt as a way of being superior to another person. We may even show a false smile to appease someone who has greater power. You can think about the major emotional expressions in terms of inherent communication signals, which are shown in the next table.[11]

Overt Expression	Goal/Intent/Communication Signal
Real smile	Interest, liking
False smile	Appeasement
Sadness	Pity
Anger	Fighting, attack, or control
Fear	Submission
Contempt	Superiority
Neutral face	Neutrality

If expressions are used to signal an intention, they can provide a clear indication of what the stated goals are, particularly if the expression is communicated in a way that is meant to be seen. We should pay attention to highly exaggerated expressions because they may say more about what a person is trying to convey than what they're actually feeling. In on situation, I had an employee who came into my office displaying sadness. She was less sad than she appeared and was trying to get some time off through my pity for her.

How to Identify False Expressions

Because people express emotions they don't necessarily feel, it's important to be able to spot false expressions. Knowing that someone isn't really experiencing something can be useful for managing that individual and your interaction with them. For example, in negotiations, people will often feign certain emotions in order to get a specific outcome. They may express happiness at seeing you, act as though they want to create an exchange that is equitable, or express anger at an offer they claim is insulting. Many of these expressions may be false and are expressed for a reason. Knowing that a person isn't really feeling something that is being expressed provides you with a view into what their motivations may be, and that can be used to your advantage. For example, if you realize that the person isn't really angry about an offer that you just suggested, then your next offer doesn't need to be much higher.

In general, expressions that are not felt can be identified by the following behaviors:[12]

- An expression that doesn't use all the muscles in the face typically associated with that expression. For example, a smile that doesn't use the eye muscles isn't a felt smile. It's very difficult to voluntarily control all the muscles associated with a felt expression and to accurately portray something one doesn't actually feel. Try it in the mirror and you'll see what I mean.
- Asymmetrical expressions also tend to be false because almost all expressions are symmetrical. The one exception to this rule is contempt, which is the only facial expression that is asymmetrical.
- An expression that is unusually long in duration (more than five to ten seconds) is typically not felt. Most facial expressions last for only a few seconds. For example, if that look of surprise stays on the face for more than a few seconds, it is most likely false.

Gender Differences in Emotional Expression

It's commonly believed that women are more "emotional" and more expressive than men by people from many different cultures.[12] However, these beliefs are emotion specific; women are thought to express more happiness, embarrassment, shame, surprise, sadness, fear and guilt than men. In contrast, men are believed to express more anger, contempt and pride than women.[13] These stereotypes tend to be supported by actual self-reports of expression by males and females. It's important to keep in mind, however, that emotional expressions don't always correspond with internal feelings. Researchers have found that men and women express different intensities of emotion, but actually feel the same level of emotion internally in response to evocative films.[14] Thus, men and women may have the same feelings but express the emotions that are most gender-appropriate.

In professional situations, there is even greater pressure to adhere to these gender display rules, which encourage women to show positive emotions and suppress negative ones, particularly anger. Men, in contrast are expected to suppress positive emotions and encouraged to display negative ones.[15] In a study of over 1,300 people in the United States, female workers reported trying to hide feelings of anger more than their male colleagues. And male workers reported trying to hide feelings of happiness more than their female colleagues.[16] The term used to describe these displays is called *emotional labor*, and it refers to expressing an emotion that isn't felt, exaggerating one that is felt, or suppressing an emotion completely. Not surprisingly, having to engage in this type of emotional labor is inherently stressful[17]. So when decoding the expressions of men and women, be aware of the expectations for male and female emotional expressivity, especially regarding anger and happiness. Women are likely to under-express negative emotions such as anger, whereas men are likely to under-express positive emotions such as happiness. In order to gauge the internal experience of these emotions, one will need to look at the microexpressions and other aspects of body language.

Some Things to Think About

In general, you will want to keep several things in mind when observing the emotional expressions of those around you in the workplace.

- What are the display rules for this workplace? What emotional expressions are expected in this particular situation? Knowing which expressions are expected can reveal a great deal when you see expressions that are unexpected. If people are expected to display understanding and helpfulness, then observing expressions that fit with these display rules may reveal little about those who express them. However, if a person displays expressions that are not consistent with expected display rules, these expressions probably reveal what he is actually feeling.

- What are the goals of people in different interactions? Knowing that people are trying to achieve certain objectives helps you perceive their expressions in light of those intentions. For example, if you know that Ross is trying to sell Amy life insurance and he expresses liking toward her and an interest in her family, you can see his emotional expressions in a different light. Expressions that are overt and in keeping with his intentions may reveal little about what he actually feels for Amy.

The Least You Need to Know

- There are seven basic emotional expressions that are recognized by people across cultures: happiness, sadness, anger, surprise, fear, disgust, and contempt.
- A real smile uses the eyes and the lips, whereas a false smile uses only the lips.
- Sadness is best identified from the eyes and eyelids. The inner corners of the eyes and eyebrows are slightly raised.
- Anger is marked by knit eyebrows and lowered eyes. The eyebrows are drawn together, sometimes creating two lines between them.
- Surprise is best identified by the raised eyes and wrinkles on the forehead.
- Fear involves the eyebrows, which are raised and may be slightly pulled together. Often the upper eyelids are raised.
- Disgust involves lowering the eyebrows and wrinkling the nose along with raising the upper lip.
- Contempt is indicated by an asymmetrical expression with one side of the lips. Contempt is typically shown by one corner of the mouth being tightened and raised slightly.
- Because overt expressions are sometimes hidden, microexpressions and partial expressions are more often observed.
- Microexpressions are expressions that occur for a very brief period and are not controlled.
- Partial expressions are expressions that are shown on only a part of the face.
- Overt expressions are sometimes shown to create a certain type of interaction with another person, and therefore they may be more a signal of people's intentions than their actual feelings.
- False expressions generally don't use all the muscles typically used for that expression, may be longer in duration than usual, and are asymmetrical (unless it is contempt).
- Women tend to be more expressive of positive emotions, particularly happiness and men tend to be more expressive of negative emotions, especially anger in professional situation. However, these expressions may not completely reflect internal feelings given cultural display rules for men and women at work.

Improving Your Ability to Read Expressions

The best way to improve your ability to read microexpressions is to receive training on them. Dr. Paul Ekman provides online training for identifying microexpressions. At the time of this publication, his website, https://www.paulekman.com/micro-expressions-training-tools/, was offering training. If you don't want to invest in online training, the exercises below will help you increase your abilities in this area.

- Stand in front of a mirror and display the following emotions: happiness, anger, sadness, contempt, surprise, fear, and disgust. Become familiar with your own expressions and what the differences are between the basic ones in terms of which parts of the face are used for each one.
- Ask someone you know well to show happiness, anger, sadness, contempt, surprise, and disgust. Ask them to display an expression and then guess which is displayed.
- Find a video interview in which the interviewer discusses some difficult topics, such as a celebrity talking about her personal life or a person discussing criminal charges against him. Any interview that covers something that is problematic for someone to discuss should suffice. Watch the interview and notice if any microexpressions appear, particularly during difficult moments. Pay close attention. Now replay the recording in slow motion and see any microexpressions you may have missed.
- Videotape yourself talking about a variety of topics—some that are difficult to discuss and others that are not. Note any microexpressions or partial expressions that appeared on your face when you watch the recording at a slower speed. What were you thinking and feeling at the time the expression was occurring on your face? Analyze your own behavior as a way to gain insight into when microexpressions and partial expressions appear on other people's faces.

References

1. Ekman, P. (2003). *Emotions revealed*. New York: Henry Holt.
2. Ekman, P. (2003). *Emotions revealed*. New York: Henry Holt.
3. Ekman, P. (2003). *Emotions revealed*. New York: Henry Holt.
4. Ekman, P., Davidson, R. J., & Friesen, W. V. (1990). Emotional expression and brain physiology II: The Duchenne smile. *Journal of Personality and Social Psychology, 58,* 342–353.
5. Ekman, P. (1992). *Telling lies*. New York: W. W. Norton.
6. Frank, M. G., & Ekman P. (1997). The ability to detect deceit generalizes across different types of high-stake lies. *Journal of Personality and Social Psychology, 72,* 1429–1439.
7. Blesch, C. (2005). 3.5 million from Homeland Security for lie detection in the 21st century. www.cs.rutgers.edu/common/apps/webarch/data/CWvueDhgIMUsMvtZkyri/
8. Donovan P. (2006). Lying is exposed by micro-expressions we can't control. www.buffalo.edu/news/fast-execute.cgi/article-page.html?article=79300009.
9. Gladwell, M. (2002). The naked face. *The New Yorker.* www.gladwell.com.
10. Ekman, P. (2003). *Emotions revealed*. New York: Henry Holt.
11. Fridlund, A. J., & Russell, J. A. (2006). The functions of facial expressions. In V. Manusov & M. Patterson (Eds.), *The Sage handbook of nonverbal communication.* Thousand Oaks, CA: Sage Publications.
12. Brody, L.R., Hall, J.A., & Stokes, L. R. (2016). Gender and emotion: theory, findings, and context. In *Handbook of Emotions*, 4th Edition. New York: Guilford Press.
13. Hess, U., Senecal, S., Kirouac, G. Herrera, P., Philippot, P., & Kleck, R.E. (2000). Emotional expressivity in men and women: Stereotypes and self-perceptions. *Cognition and Emotion,* 14, 609–642.
14. Kring, A. M., & Gordon, A. H. (1998). Sex differences in emotion: Expression, experience and physiology. *Journal of Personality and Social Psychology,* 74 686-703.
15. Brody, L.R., Hall, J.A., & Stokes, L. R. (2016). Gender and emotion: theory, findings, and context. In *Handbook of Emotions*, 4th Edition. New York: Guilford Press.
16. Sloane, M. M. (2012). Controlling anger and happiness at work: An examination of gender differences. *Gender, Work and Organization,* 19, 370-391.

17. Brody, L.R., Hall, J.A., & Stokes, L. R. (2016). Gender and emotion: theory, findings, and context. In *Handbook of Emotions*, 4th Edition. New York: Guilford Press.

CHAPTER 4: CONTACT

> **Some Basic Ideas:**
>
> In general, people tend to touch those whom they like and feel comfortable with. Touching reveals feelings and increases as relationships become closer.
>
> Touching is more likely to occur when people are trying to persuade others, when people are higher in status, and when they have certain personality attributes like extroversion.

The word *contact* refers to physical contact, which is an essential part of human life. Interestingly, touch is critical to human development as the medical community in Europe learned during World War II. The death rate of babies was extremely high in orphanages even though the babies were well cared for in terms of their basic needs (e.g., food, shelter, and clothing). The babies were only touched, however, when someone was feeding or bathing them. It was only when older women were hired to hold and rock the babies that the death rate dropped to almost zero.[1] Apparently the need for touching in humans is so great that without it, babies will perish.

Different cultures vary in the amount of physical contact that is acceptable. In a study conducted in the 1960s, a researcher counted how many times couples in cafés touched each other in four different cities.[2] In Puerto Rico the couples touched each other on average about 180 times. In Paris they touched 110 times, in Florida they touched twice, and in London they didn't touch at all. Asian cultures are believed to be even less tactile than American and European cultures.

North American society is typically described as a *noncontact* culture where there are strong norms against touching others. Some people have suggested that we address our needs for contact by hiring "licensed touchers." Examples of these individuals include masseuses, chiropractors, and hairdressers. Although North

American culture may not be highly tactile, we do have physical contact with one another and the type of contact we have can be very revealing. We first discuss the most common form of touching at work: the handshake.

What Handshakes Reveal

In most professional situations, the first type of physical contact we have with someone is the handshake. The American handshake is typically firm and includes two and a half shakes. The handshake has an interesting history because it originated in early cultures and was a sign that neither person had weapons in his hands. It was a way of showing that the interaction was peaceful. It is probably because of this history that men shook hands long before women began to do so.

What can you tell from someone's handshake? Although some people believe that one can judge another's personality attributes from a handshake, it's not been established that the scripted handshake reveals a great deal about a person. We know that people are perceived negatively when they engage in the *dead-fish* handshake or in the *bone-crushing* handshake. But personality isn't easily discerned from just a handshake.

The reason why the handshake tells you very little is that it is socially prescribed and people are just following social norms. Thus, watching David shake Carol's hand doesn't tell you much about David. However, if David deviates from the norm and refuses to shake hands with Carol, his behavior either tells you about his feelings for Carol or shows that he doesn't understand the social norms. Touch avoidance can also be indicative of a psychological problem or a disease, which I discuss later.

The handshake, however, can sometimes reveal the closeness of a relationship between two people. According to Desmond Morris, one can tell the strength of the connection between two people who are shaking hands by observing the hand that isn't involved in the handshake.[3] If the relationship is close, the other hand may extend toward the other person. If the relationship isn't close, the non-shaking hand may hang limply at the side of the body. You can also tell about the degree of connection from the proximity of the two people during a handshake. As previously discussed, we tend to stand nearer those whom we like. Look at the next photos. In the first photo, the women are standing closer together. In the next photo, they're further apart. Although they have similar expressions on their faces, you get a very different feeling about the nature of their relationship from the second photo. They look like acquaintances in the first photo and like friends in the second one.

Contact Reveals Type of Relationship

Although the handshake is the most common form of touching, particularly if we don't know someone well, there are other types of touching that are common in professional situations. Touching in the workplace tends to occur above the waist and is directed toward the *hands, arms,* and *back.* These forms of unscripted touching outside the handshake are the most revealing.

In general, we know that touching outside of the handshake reveals positive feelings about the other person. Generally the more we like someone, the more we tend to touch them. However, we generally will not deviate from the acceptable places of touching such as the back, arms, and hands. In addition, the more comfortable we are with someone, the more we tend to touch them. Thus, if someone touches your arm during a meeting, the person initiating the physical contact is communicating a comfort and degree of liking that says he feels comfortable enough to touch you and assumes you will not be offended. The more we dislike someone, the less we tend to touch him.

The amount of touching that you observe between two people indicates the nature of their relationship. Physical contact varies on a continuum and reveals four types of relationships:[4] 1) functional/professional, 2) social/polite, 3) friendship/warmth, and 4) love/intimacy. Touching occurs least in the functional/professional and social/polite relationships. Examples of functional/professional relationships include interactions with physicians, hairdressers, and cashiers—people who touch us as part of their jobs. It is a socially acceptable form of touching. Social/polite touching occurs between people who don't know one another well or who have just been introduced. This type of touch is restricted to the handshake. And in some cultures (not North American culture), this touching will also include a quick kiss on the cheek or a momentary hug. In both of these situations, the amount of touching is indicative of a fairly formal relationship that isn't close.

As we progress along the continuum of relationships, the next two types are friendship/warmth and love/intimacy. Relationships that are classified as friendship/warmth have touching that falls outside of the formal handshake. Examples include patting on the back and touching the arm or shoulder. It's important to watch touching behavior because it tells you how people feel about you. For example, I always notice when clients start to touch me outside of the social/polite touching because it tells me that they view me more as a friend than as a vendor. So, when a client pats me on the back or gives me a momentary hug upon meeting, I know that we've moved into a friendship/warmth relationship.

The last type of relationship is the love/intimacy one. This type of relationship doesn't need to be explained in terms of touching. One interesting finding is that in long-term relationships, touching tends to decline over time. Touching tends to peak for couples as they approach the most intimate phases of their relationships and then to level off over time.[5] Some psychologists have suggested that touching may be essential for the creation of a love relationship but may be less necessary for maintaining one.[6] By observing a couple one may have a sense of where they are in the creation or maintenance of a love relationship just by their touching behavior.

Touching Reveals Emotions

Physical contact also conveys what people are feeling. This research is some of the more interesting work and involves asking people to communicate certain feelings by only touching another person's arm. The person expressing the emotion is seated behind an opaque black curtain and only her hands and arms can be seen. Researchers found that people are able to accurately express the emotions of anger, disgust, fear, love, gratitude and sympathy just by touching another person's arm. [7,8] And touch is even more effective at expressing emotions when one is touching areas of the body in addition to the arm. That touch can communicate so many feelings is not surprising, and it makes reading this particular nonverbal behavior important. Interestingly there is cross-cultural similarity in the emotions that can be read through physical contact[9].

Types of Touching in the Workplace

The various forms of touching that occur in the workplace can be described in the following five types: 1) positive-affect touches, 2) playful touches, 3) control touches, 4) ritualistic touches, and 5) task-oriented touches.[10] Positive-affect touches refer to touches that express some degree of liking for another person and express things like comfort, appreciation, support, affection, and so on. Playful touches are joking behaviors such as play fighting or tickling and shoving. These types of touches would be very unusual in the workplace, but if they occur, they denote a very strong friendship between people. Control touches are those that are intended to influence a person or to get his attention. Ritualistic touching refers to handshakes that are common during greetings and departures. Task-oriented touches occur during situations that require them, such as helping someone out of a car or handing someone something. Obviously the most common type of touching in the workplace would be ritualistic and task-oriented touching. Other types of touching such as positive-affect and playful touching are less common and denote a close relationship.

Interestingly, touching increases as situations become more emotional. In personal relationships, we will sometimes offer comfort by touching someone when she is distressed. And we know that as conversations deepen, people are more likely to touch their conversational partners.[11] In airports, 60 percent of those who are saying hello or good-bye touch the other person.[12] Clearly these situations can be highly emotional. In work situations, the comforting someone through touching indicates that the relationship has progressed from a professional to personal relationship.

Contact Reveals Status and a Desire to Influence

We are also more likely to be touched in situations in which someone has higher status and is giving information, advice, or orders.[13] What's interesting is that people are less likely to touch you if they're asking for advice or information, or receiving orders. In this situation, the lower-status position doesn't tend to initiate touching. In the next photo you can imagine that the man on the left is giving some type of advice or instructing his subordinate about what he needs to do. I suspect that he feels comfortable enough to touch his colleague because he has the dominant position.

In general, those who are higher in status are more likely to touch those who are lower in status rather than vice versa.[14] So if Cindy is the supervisor, she is more likely to touch her subordinate, Jeff, than he is to touch her. This difference in touching may be caused by a variety of factors, including comfort and familiarity. Those who are in positions of authority may feel more comfortable in those interactions than their subordinates. Interestingly, regardless of who is touching whom, people tend to believe the person who is touched has lower status than the person who initiates the physical contact.

One can identify differences in status by observing who initiates touch and whether it's reciprocated. I always watch people when they interact with one another in work settings to see who touches whom. At one of my client companies I observed a high-level manager touching a subordinate on the shoulder as he told her what he wanted her to do on a project. His touch told me that he was higher in status than she was, and that he was telling her what to do rather than asking her for her thoughts.

People are also more likely to touch you when they are trying to persuade you of something or when asking for a favor. Interestingly research has shown that people are more likely to comply with requests if they're touched during an appeal. In one study, shoppers in a supermarket were approached and asked to sample a new food product. Half of the shoppers were touched when they were asked to sample the product and the other half weren't. Those who were touched were more likely to sample and purchase the new food even though both groups rated the product equally on taste.[15] And in one of my favorite studies, people give a larger tip to a waitress if she touched the customer when giving change.[16] Touching a person while asking for something is probably a learned behavior that people don't even realize they're doing. Because it works, it's probably second nature to do it. But we're less likely to touch others if we are agreeing to do a favor or when we're being persuaded. So the next time someone asks you for something and touches you, consider that their touch is a signal of their desire to influence you more than it is a sign of their affection for you.

Gender Differences in Touching and Perceptions of Touch

Which gender do you think initiates the most touching—men or women? If you guessed women, you're correct. Women initiate touch more than men. One of the reasons women touch more is because there are cultural norms against men touching each other. One exception is during team sports—either watching or playing them. It's considered perfectly acceptable for football players to pat each other on the backside or for men watching or playing a game to give high-fives—slapping hands up high. See the next photos for examples. Another appropriate moment of touching between men is during roughhousing.[17] It's perfectly acceptable for men to mock fight and for one man to grasp another man's head in the crook of his arm. One reason for men's lack of touching may be that they fear it will be perceived as an indication that they are gay. Men who dislike same-sex touching the most tend to have the most anti-gay attitudes.[18]

So women touch others more than men do, primarily because women touch both genders. But women also receive touch more than men. Women tend to find touching more pleasant than men.[19] This attitude toward touching may be part of the reason women are touched more often; they like it. Women may also be perceived as less threatening than men and people may feel greater comfort touching women than touching men. What's interesting is that women and men tend to touch differently.[20] Women are more likely to show affection by hugging, kissing, and touching to show support. As previously mentioned, men are more likely to engage in playful touching (such as mock fighting or teasing). Thus, when you're interpreting touch from another person, consider the norms for the gender of the person touching you. A man who engages in playful touching and a woman who hugs you may be saying the same thing but in different ways because of gender norms.

Physical Contact Can Reveal Personality Attributes

People who are extroverted and self-confident tend to touch others more than those who aren't high on these personality attributes.[21] Extroverted, self-confident individuals, as previously discussed, show nonverbal behavior that is different from that of introverted people. One reason for these differences may be that extroverted people like interacting with others and touching can be part of the interaction. They also may not experience anxiety when interacting with others and therefore feel more comfortable in social situations to touch others. People who touch others the least tend to report more anxiety and tension in their lives, tend to be more socially withdrawn, and tend to have lower satisfaction with their bodies.[22, 23]

Individuals who prefer not to initiate or receive touch are called *touch avoidant*. There are numerous reasons for this avoidance. For some people touching is physically painful because of an illness or injury. Some of the people in my seminars have told me that arthritis has made it very difficult for them to shake another person's hand because it hurts them. Some people have phobias about germs and catching diseases from touching others, which is clearly a psychological problem. However, barring physiological issues or cleanliness phobias, touch avoidance is associated with certain personality attributes and with religious affiliation, age, and marital status.[24] In personality assessments of touch avoiders, researchers have found that those who are touch avoidant tend to be more shy, emotionally fragile, and socially withdrawn than those who aren't touch avoidant.[25] Apparently, people from the northern Midwest, Northern Europe, Asia, Canada, and Australia are more likely to be touch avoidant than people from the Mediterranean or the Caribbean.[26] Women from Muslim and Hindu countries and fundamentalist Protestant men and women as well as Orthodox Jews are more likely to be touch avoiders.[27] Older people are more likely to be touch avoidant than younger people, and married individuals are more likely to be touch avoidant than single people.[28] About 20 percent of North Americans are classified as touch avoidant.[29]

I'm intrigued by people who are touch avoidant. If a person avoids touching only me, that tells me they don't like me. However, if he is touch avoidant with only certain groups, that can reveal discomfort or prejudice toward that group. If he is touch avoidant with all people, then I assume that his avoidance is due to a physical or emotional issue. Generally his other behaviors will be indicative of what's going on. If the person is extroverted in many ways except when it comes to touch, then there may be a physical issue (such as arthritis) rather than an emotional one. However, if the person is somewhat avoidant toward people in general, then this person may have psychological issues.

Some Things to Think About

There are certain things you should consider when observing physical contact:
- Watch touching that occurs outside the handshake. This touching is the most revealing because it's unscripted.
- Watch any touching that occurs outside of touching on the hands, arms, and back. Touching outside these areas is very unusual in the workplace and suggests an intimate relationship.
- Keep in mind that people differ in terms of how much they like touching. Some people are very tactile, so their touching may be less revealing than that of individuals who are less tactile.

The Least You Need to Know

- In general, people tend to touch those whom they like and feel most comfortable with.
- The handshake can sometimes reveal the closeness of a relationship between two people. If the relationship is a close one, the non-shaking hand may extend toward the other person and the two people may stand close together.
- Touch reveals the type of relationship people have with one another. A greater amount of touch occurs as relationships become closer. The least amount of touch occurs in the functional/professional relationship, and the most occurs in friendship/warmth and love/intimacy relationships.
- Touch reveals feelings. People are able to accurately express the emotions of anger, disgust, fear, love, gratitude and sympathy just by touching another person's arm.

- The most common types of touches in the workplace are ritualistic and task-oriented touches.
- People are more likely to touch those whom they are trying to persuade or influence, or who are lower in status than them.
- Women tend to initiate and receive the most touch.
- There are cultural norms against men touching one another except in certain situations (for example, team sports) and in certain ways (for example, roughhousing).
- Extroverted, self-confident people tend to touch people more often than those who are introverted.
- Individuals who prefer not to initiate or receive touch are called *touch avoidant,* which can be caused by physical or psychological issues. Touch avoidance can also be associated with certain religious, age, and marital groups.

Improving Your Ability to Read Physical Contact

All too often we don't observe touching because it occurs quickly and is scripted. However, for the next several days, pay attention to several aspects of touching to improve your ability to read physical contact.

- ○ Notice when people shake hands how much distance there is between them. Notice what the other hand is doing at the time of the handshake. Can you tell something about how the individuals feel about one another from just watching their handshake?
- ○ Observe unscripted touch (touching outside of handshakes). Whom does it tend to occur between? Is it reciprocated? What does this touching tell you about the nature of the relationship between the two people?
- ○ Observe when unscripted touch occurs toward you. Does it tend to happen in certain circumstances—when people are trying to persuade you of something or when asking a favor?
- ○ Keep a touching diary of all the people you touch and who touches you in professional interactions (outside the handshake). Note the following items:
  - ○ Who touched whom
  - ○ Whether it was reciprocated
  - ○ Gender of person who initiated
  - ○ Situation

- o Type of relationship (such as colleague, subordinate, client, customer, and so on)
- o Is there a pattern of touching in your life?

References

1. Richmond, V. P., & McCroskey, J. C. (2000). *Nonverbal behavior in interpersonal relations*. Needham Heights, MA: Allyn & Bacon.
2. Jourard, S. M. (1966). An exploratory study of body accessibility. *British Journal of Social and Clinical Psychology, 26*, 235–242.
3. Morris D. (1971). *Intimate behavior*. New York: Random House.
4. Richmond, V. P., & McCroskey, J. C. (2000). *Nonverbal behavior in interpersonal relations*. Needham Heights, MA: Allyn & Bacon.
5. Emmers, T. M., & Dindia, K. (1995). The effect of relational stage and intimacy on touch: An extension of Guerrero and Anderson. *Personal Relationships, 2*, 225–236.
6. Anderson, P. A., Guerrero, L. K., & Jones, S. M. (2006). Nonverbal behavior in intimate interactions and intimate relationships. In V. Manusov & M. Patterson (Eds.), *The Sage handbook of nonverbal communication*. Thousand Oaks, CA: Sage Publications.
7. Hertenstein, M. J., Keltner, D., App, B., Bulleit, B. A., & Jaskolka, A. R. (2006). Touch communicates distinct emotions. *Emotion, 6*(3) 528.
8. Hertenstein, M. J., Holmes, R., McCullough, M., & Keltner D. (2009). The communication of emotion via touch. *Emotion, 9*(4), 566.
9. Hertenstein, M. J., Holmes, R., McCullough, M., & Keltner D. (2009). The communication of emotion via touch. *Emotion, 9*(4), 566.
10. Burgoon, J. K., Buller, D. B., & Woodall, W. K., (1996). *Nonverbal Communication*. New York: McGraw-Hill
11. Knapp, M. L., & Hall, J. H. (2002). *Nonverbal communication in human interaction*. Belmont, CA: Thomson Learning.
12. Greenbaum, P. E., & Rosenfeld, H. M. (1980). Varieties of touching in greetings: Sequential structure and sex-related differences. *Journal of Nonverbal Behavior, 5*, 13–25.
13. Henley, N. M. (1977). *Body politics: Power, sex and nonverbal communication*. Englewood Cliffs, NJ: Prentice-Hall.
14. Hall, J. A. (1996). Touch, status and gender at professional meetings. *Journal of Nonverbal Behavior, 20*, 23–44.

15. Smith, D. E., Gier, J. A., & Willis, F. N. (1982). Interpersonal touch and compliance with a marketing request. *Basic and Applied Social Psychology, 3* (1), 35–38.

16. Crusco, A. H., & Wetzel, C. G. (2008). The Midas touch: The effects of interpersonal touch on restaurant tipping. In L. K. Guerrero & M. L. Hecht (Eds.), *The Nonverbal Communication Reader*. Long Grove, IL: Waveland Press.

17. Morris, D. (1971). *Intimate behavior*. New York: Random House.

18. Roese, N. J., Olson, J. M., Borenstein, M. N., Martin, A., & Shores, A. L. (1992). Same-sex touching behavior: The moderating role of homophobic attitudes. *Journal of Nonverbal Behavior, 16,* 249–259.

19. Hall. J. A. (1984). *Nonverbal sex differences: Communication accuracy and expressive style*. Baltimore: Johns Hopkins University Press.

20. Derlega, V. J., Lewis, R. J., Harrison, S., Winstead, B. A., & Constanzo, R. (1989). Gender differences in the initiation and attribution of tactile intimacy. *Journal of Nonverbal Behavior, 13,* 83–96.

21. Anderson, P. A., & Liebowitz, K. (1978). The development and nature of the construct touch avoidance. *Environmental Psychology and Nonverbal Behavior, 3,* 89–106.

22. Anderson, J. F., Anderson, P. A., & Lustig, M. W. (1987). Opposite sex touch avoidance: A national replication and extension. *Journal of Nonverbal Behavior, 11,* 89–109.

23. Deethardt, J. F., & Hines, D. G. (1983). Tactile communication and personality differences. *Journal of Nonverbal Behavior, 8,* 143–156.

24. Richmond, V. P., & McCroskey, J. C. (2000). *Nonverbal behavior in interpersonal relations*. Needham Heights, MA: Allyn & Bacon.

25. Richmond, V. P., & McCroskey, J. C. (2000). *Nonverbal behavior in interpersonal relations*. Needham Heights, MA: Allyn & Bacon.

26. Anderson, P. A. (2004). *The complete idiot's guide to body language*. New York: Alpha Books.

27. Anderson, P. A. (2004). *The complete idiot's guide to body language*. New York: Alpha Books.

28. Anderson, P. A. (2004). *The complete idiot's guide to body language*. New York: Alpha Books.

29. Richmond, V. P., & McCroskey, J. C. (2000). *Nonverbal behavior in interpersonal relations*. Needham Heights, MA: Allyn & Bacon.

CHAPTER 5: EYES

Some Basic Ideas:

In general, people tend to look more frequently and for longer duration at those whom they like and who have engaged their attention.

People tend to look more at higher-status people than lower-status ones.

Eye behavior reveals when something is cognitively complex or emotionally difficult to discuss.

Eye behavior can also reveal personality attributes. Those who are shy and socially anxious, or who have low self-esteem and negative feelings about themselves, tend to spend less time looking at others.

There are gender and racial differences in looking that should be considered when interpreting eye behavior.

It has been said that the eyes are the window to the soul. If ever there was a window to the inner life of a person, I think the eyes are a good place to start. Because the eyes are a major way we take in much of our information about the world, our eye behavior reveals when we're interested in people and things, whom we like, and when we don't want to interact with others. The eyes also tell us when things are cognitively complicated or emotionally difficult for a person to discuss.

The Eyes Reveal Interest and Liking

Generally, we look longer and more frequently at people and things that have our attention. That point seems almost intuitively obvious given that we rely on our sight probably more than any other sense when we're gathering information about the world. We reveal if we're engaged with a presentation by how much we view its content. We reveal how interested we are in another person by how much we look at him while he's talking. In one study researchers found that people tend to gaze more at someone who is giving them positive feedback but that they reduce their gaze when they're receiving negative feedback.[1] The eyes reveal how much we want to take in around us.

What's amazing about eye behavior is that we secretly reveal whom we like and dislike just by the amount that we look at a person. Aside from the intentional stare that's associated with anger and a desire for a confrontation, we generally look most at those whom we like and find rewarding. In one study, men looked more at other men with whom they had just conversed and who had nodded at them during a presentation.[2] It's unlikely that these men had formed strong feelings of liking but that they had mildly positive feelings about the other person, and their eye behavior showed it. People avoid looking at someone who has just made negative comments about their performance and who is presumably mildly disliked.[3] Mothers of children who have temperament problems actually look less at their problematic children.[4]

As people increase their liking for one another, they increase the amount of mutual gazing that they do. (Mutual gaze is when two people are looking into each other's eyes). The most obvious example of this occurs along the continuum of relationships. We don't look for long periods at strangers, but we clearly engage in mutual gaze with our good friends. Romantic relationships have the highest amount of mutual gaze.

Gazing also reveals prejudices. In a study of racial prejudice, researchers had people interview with Caucasian or African American interviewers. Interviewees who were prejudiced toward African Americans actually gazed less at the interviewer if he was African American.[5] Of course, they didn't know they were looking less at the interviewer or that their attitudes about an entire race were being betrayed by their eyes. But their eyes revealed the truth.

In general, we tend to look at others about half the time we're with them, particularly in one-on-one interactions. People tend to gaze more while listening than while talking. In general, people tend to look at others for about three seconds at a time. The amount of time that we engage in mutual eye contact (both partners looking at each other at the same time) is about 1.2 seconds.[6] If looking behavior is longer or shorter than these intervals, it reveals the level of interest and liking. A gaze of ten seconds or longer will produce irritation, and very long gazes are associated with anger. However, looking frequently at another person for three to five seconds is generally indicative of liking and engagement. Gazing for a shorter period of time is indicative of dislike or disinterest.

In a meeting where a colleague and I were presenting our services to a potential client, I noticed that the prospective client looked more frequently and for longer duration at a colleague than me. I realized that the potential client seemed more interested and engaged with my associate, so I took a backseat in the meeting and let him take over. We later learned that the potential client is the head of an all-male department and has difficulty relating to female employees and suppliers. His discomfort was shown by his eye behavior, and it helped us to tailor the dynamics of the meeting and eventually to do a project for this individual. I decided not to be involved with him or with the project.

Eye Behaviors Reveal Who Has High Status and Who Has Low Status

People tend to look more at those who are higher in status than those who are lower. Thus, in professional meetings you should expect that the leader will receive more gaze from her subordinates than she gives to them. An interesting part of this dynamic is that people who are higher in status (or dominance) tend to look more when speaking than when listening. In contrast, people who are lower in status tend look more when listening than when they're speaking.[7,8] It's possible that when we have a role (or personality attributes) that accords us a certain status, we engage with others in a way that we expect them to listen to us. Looking at someone while we're talking is a clear indication of our expectation that the person should listen.

One can see who has status at meetings by observing how much people look at the individuals at the table. At one meeting I attended, there were two individuals at the table whom I identified as having the most status in the organization. The first person, Jim, sat at the head of the table and directed the meeting. The other person was a man named Sanjay who sat at the middle of the table. When Sanjay spoke, people gazed attentively at him and listened to whatever he said. And this included Jim, who ran the meeting. I learned later that Jim had a significant title in the organization but that Sanjay has tremendous expertise and is highly valued by his colleagues and managers. The other people at the table told me how much power Jim and Sanjay have with their eyes.

Another interesting aspect of eye behavior is the role that it plays in regulating interactions and conversation.[9,10] Human beings use their eyes to communicate who will speak next. The typical pattern is as follows. The speaker finishes her thought and then looks at the listener until that person starts speaking. The new speaker will then maintain gaze with the previous speaker until it is established that he is now in the speaking role. Then she will look away. In small groups, leaders tend to engage in prolonged eye contact with someone at the end of their speech, which is a way of inviting that person to start speaking. Leaders, therefore, are not just speaking but also controlling who talks and when that occurs with their eyes. In the example I just mentioned, Jim often gave Sanjay the floor with his eye behavior, which is one of the ways that he encouraged Sanjay's participation in the meeting.

Eye Behavior Reveals Cognitive Complexity and Emotional Difficulty

One of the more fascinating aspects of eye behavior is that it reveals when a person is thinking of something that is cognitively complex. Try this exercise at some point. Ask someone what 9 x 13 equals and see if he glances away to make the calculation. When he arrives at a number, he should look back at you. Looking away shows a shift from external things to internal thinking. It also indicates an effort to block out external stimulation so one can do the calculation without interference. Interestingly, people tend to glance away when they're answering questions that are more difficult to answer and that require some level of reflection. (For example, which is farther east: Nashville or Indianapolis?) Apparently, looking away helps people answer questions more accurately. When people are required to answer a question either with their eyes closed or while directly looking at another person, they answer more accurately when their eyes are closed.[11]

If people don't close their eyes when they're answering a cognitively complex question, they tend to look either to the right or to the left.[12] The side where one tends to glance reflects which hemisphere of the brain is being used. Those who glance to the right are accessing the left hemisphere and those who are glancing to the left are accessing the right hemisphere. The left hemisphere is associated with intellectual and linguistic tasks, whereas the right hemisphere involves spatial or emotional processing.[13,14] People who tend to glance to the left tend to be less analytical, more involved with feelings, more creative, and more susceptible to hypnosis than those who tend to glance to the right.[15]

Glancing away while talking can also indicate when something is emotionally difficult to discuss. Looking away is another mechanism people use to regulate their thoughts and emotions. You'll notice that if something is difficult to talk about, you will tend to look away from someone while speaking about it, particularly if it's something you're ashamed of or if its emotionally evocative. In one study, when participants failed at a task and were publicly criticized, they reported feeling embarrassed, and the amount of gazing that they did toward others diminished.[16] Identifying the things that are emotionally difficult for another person through eye behavior can provide insight into the things that matter and the issues or topics that are difficult to discuss. A life-insurance salesman once told me that he asks prospects emotionally evocative questions so he can identify areas that are painful for them. When he hits on something that someone has difficulty talking about, he sells his services around these areas of pain. It's certainly something to keep in mind if you're in sales or if you're at the receiving end of a sales pitch.

Eye Behavior Reveals Personality Attributes and Competition

Not surprisingly one's eye behavior is related to one's personality. People who are shy or socially anxious spend less time looking at others. Gazing at others may invite interaction, which may be unwelcome. In general, people who spend the most time looking at others tend to have one of the following needs:[17,18]

- A high need for interaction, inclusion, or affiliation with one or more people. People who want to be involved with another person or included with a group of people tend to look at others more and to return gazing from others.
- A high need for information and feedback. People tend to look more to others to gauge how others are responding to them.
- A desire to persuade someone of something

Those who spend the least time looking at others tend to:

- have low self-esteem or negative feelings about themselves;
- have a lesser desire to interact with others because of a negative perception of other people;
- be negatively aroused by looking at others and by being gazed at by others. Children with autism are an example of people who can find gaze upsetting. Shy people can also find the potential interaction from gazing upsetting.

By watching the eye behavior of others, you can get a glimpse of some enduring personality traits as well as needs for affiliation (or lack thereof).

Interestingly, people tend to use their eyes differently when they're competing versus cooperating with another person.[19] In one study, researchers found that people who are cooperating tend to look longer at one another and to use mutual gazing to indicate their liking, honesty, and trustworthiness. In contrast, competitors tended to look at their rivals frequently and for short durations. The researchers believe that competitors are sizing up their partner's performance and intentions without giving away any information about themselves.

Gender, Racial and Cultural Differences in Eye Behavior

Women and men differ in the amount of gazing they give and receive from others. Women look at others during interactions much more than men. Women's gazing is longer, more frequent, and more reciprocal than men's.[20] These gender differences have been observed across the life span from infancy to old age. Female babies and children gaze at others more than male babies and children. And women receive more gazing from others than men. As a result of these gender differences, mutual gaze is higher between two women than it is between two men. For interactions that occur between women and men, the amount of gaze is intermediate. Thus, the highest rates of gazing occur in the following order:

- o Female-to-female interactions (most gazing)
- o Female-to-male interactions (intermediate gazing)
- o Male-to-male interactions (least gazing)

Thus, women are the object and the initiators of the most gazing behavior. As a result, female-female interactions are likely to be the most intimate and male-male interactions are likely to be the least intimate in terms of eye behavior. These different gender norms for gazing are important to consider when interpreting the eye behavior of men and women. Given that women tend to look at others more than men, women may appear more interested and engaged with others than they actually are, and men may appear to be less interested and engaged than they actually are.

Another major difference in eye behavior occurs with regard to race. Caucasians tend to gaze more at their conversational partners while listening than do African Americans.[21] Some African Americans may even consider it inappropriate or impolite to engage in frequent eye contact when they're listening. Theorists have speculated that these different levels of eye contact may be a carryover from eye-contact norms in Africa, where children are not permitted to look at an adult directly. Caucasians and African Americans also differ in terms of their eye behavior when they're speaking.[22,23] It's conventional for white individuals to look intermittently at their listener, particularly when they're emphasizing a point. In contrast, African Americans tend to look steadily at listeners while they're speaking. These different eye behaviors may cause Caucasians to view African Americans as inattentive when listening and potentially as intimidating when talking. African Americans, in contrast, may view white speakers as intimidating when listening and as inattentive to them when they're talking. Both of these conclusions are incorrect, but they could be inferred given the current eye-behavior norms for each racial group.

And culture also influences eye behavior[24]. People from Latin America, the Middle East and Southern Europe tend to look directly at a listener while speaking. In contrast, Asians, Indians, Pakistanis and Northern Europeans tend to look less directly at a listener, or not at all, as a way of showing respect[25]. One can imagine how many times conversational partners from two different cultures have incorrect perceptions of one another as a result of these customs.

The Least You Need to Know

- o People tend to look more frequently and for longer durations at those whom they like and who have engaged their attention.
- o People look less at people whom they dislike and for whom they have negative prejudicial attitudes.
- o Higher-status people tend to be looked at more than lower-status individuals.
- o Higher-status people and those who are high in dominance tend to look more while they're speaking than when they're listening to others.
- o Eye behavior reveals when something is emotionally difficult or cognitively complex. People tend to glance away when doing a complex task or when discussing something that's emotionally difficult.
- o Eye behavior can also reveal personality attributes. Individuals who are shy or socially anxious, or who have low self-esteem and negative feelings about themselves, spend less time looking at others.
- o Those who spend a lot of time looking at others tend to have a high need for interaction with others or a strong desire for information and feedback.
- o The most gazing occurs between two women, the least gazing occurs between two men, and an intermediate amount occurs between a man and a woman.
- o Caucasians tend to look at their conversational partners more than African Americans while listening. And when speaking, African Americans tend to look at their conversational partners more than Caucasians.

Some Things to Think About

When thinking about eye behavior in professional situations, it's useful to divide it into two categories: 1) when you're speaking and 2) when the other person is speaking. If you're speaking and receiving little or no eye contact from the listener, it's generally for one of the following reasons:

- The person isn't interested in what you're saying.
- The person is thinking about something else.
- The person doesn't like you.
- You have lower status than this person.
- The person has low self-esteem.
- The person is introverted and has a low need for interaction.
- Racial, ethnicity or cultural gazing norms are different from your own.
- Gender norms are different from those of your gender.

If the person is talking to you and giving you little or no eye contact, it is likely for one of the following reasons:

- The topic is cognitively complex.
- The topic is emotionally difficult.
- The person doesn't like you.
- The person has low self-esteem or is introverted.
- Racial, ethnicity or cultural norms are different from your own.
- Gender norms are different from those of your gender.

Eye behavior during meetings is particularly interesting because you can determine who likes whom and who has the most status just from the eyes. You can also determine who gives whom permission to speak. Recall that high-status people tend to signal when another person can speak through prolonged eye contact at the end of their utterances. Thus, you can see how the baton is passed just by watching people's eyes. You can also see who has the most respect in a room by the amount of eye contact they're given. If everyone is attentive when Maria speaks and all eyes are on her, it's clear she has the respect of the group. If people are looking at their neighbors, their notebooks, and around the room when Daryl speaks, the lack of respect he's accorded is shown by his colleagues' eyes. In the end, the eyes have it.

Improving Your Ability to Read the Eyes

Because eye behavior is fast and fleeting, it's easy to overlook—literally. However, our gazing is an important indicator of many of our thoughts and feelings about others. Others' gazing behavior is a good indicator of their thoughts and feelings about us and how they feel about what we're saying. For the next few days spend some time looking at others' eye behavior.

- o Watch a movie that has characters who vary in terms of how much they like one another. Note the amount of time they tend to spend looking at one another. Count the seconds and note how frequently they tend to look at one another. Do people who supposedly like one another look at each other more in the movies?
- o Watch people who clearly like or dislike one another and notice how much they look at one another. Does eye behavior reveal liking?
- o Observe how boring versus interesting topics influence eye behavior. Do people look at you less when you're being entertaining than when you're not? Try this experiment with a close friend. Talk about something that he finds completely boring and drone on about it. Watch his eye behavior while you're doing this, and then switch to a topic you know he wants to talk about and see the difference. How much did he look at you when you were being boring versus interesting?
- o Watch eye behavior in professional situations and observe the following:
  - o Are leaders looked at most or not?
  - o Do the most respected people get looked at the most?
  - o Does a high-status person who is liked and respected experience the most gazing from others?
- o Watch couples who have recently begun a relationship and compare their gazing behavior with those who are more established. Does it differ?
- o Watch several different dyads (two people interacting) that differ by gender and determine how much eye contact occurs.
  - o Watch two women interacting.
  - o Watch two men interacting.
  - o Watch a man and a woman interacting.

How strong are the gender norms for gazing behavior? Across several different dyads, how much did the eye behavior conform to the gender norms? If it didn't conform, what other factors influenced eye behavior?

References

1. Greene, J. O., & Frandsen, K. D. (1979). Need-fulfillment and consistency theory: Relationships between self-esteem and eye contact. *Western Journal of Speech Communication, 43*, 123–133.

2. Efran, J. S., & Broughton, A. (1966). Effect of expectancies for social approval on visual behavior. *Journal of Personality and Social Psychology, 4*, 103–107.

3. Exline, R. V., & Winters, L. (1965). Affective relations and mutual glances in dyads. In S. Tomkins & C. Izard (Eds.), *Affect, cognition and personality*. New York: Springer.

4. Knapp M. L., & Hall, J. A. (2006). *Nonverbal communication in human interaction*. Belmont, CA: Thomson Wadsworth.

5. Dovidio, J. F., Kawakami, K., Johnson, C., Johnson, B., & Howard, A. (1997). On the nature of prejudice: Automatic and controlled processes. *Journal of Experimental Social Psychology, 33*, 510–540.

6. Argyle, M., & Ingham, R. (1972). Gaze, mutual gaze and proximity. *Semiotica, 6*, 32–49.

7. LaFrance, J., & Mayo, C. (1978). *Moving bodies: Nonverbal communication in social relationships*. Monterey, CA: Brooks/Cole Publishing.

8. Patterson, M. L. (1983). *Nonverbal behavior: A functional perspective*. New York: Springer-Verlag.

9. Knapp, M. L., & Hall, J. H. (2002). *Nonverbal communication in human interaction*. Belmont, CA: Thomson Learning.

10. Kalma, A. (1992). Gazing in triads: A powerful signal in floor apportionment. *British Journal of Social Psychology, 31*, 21–39.

11. Glenberg, A. M., Schroeder, J. L., & Robertson, D. A. (1998). Averting the gaze disengages the environment and facilitates remembering. *Memory & Cognition, 26*, 651–658.

12. Bakan, P., & Strayer, F. F. (1973). On reliability of conjugate lateral eye movements. *Perceptual and Motor Skills, 36*, 429–430.

13. De Gennaro, L., & Violani, C. (1988). Reflective lateral eye movements: Individual styles, cognitive and lateralization effects. *Neuropsychologia, 26*, 727–736.

14. Weisz, J., & Adams, G. (1993). Hemispheric preference and lateral eye movements evoked by bilateral visual stimuli. *Neuropsychologia, 31*, 1299–1306.

15. Knapp, M. L., & Hall, J. H. (2002). *Nonverbal communication in human interaction*. Belmont, CA: Thomson Learning.

16. Modigliani, A. (1971). Embarrassment, facework and eye-contact: Testing a theory of embarrassment. *Journal of Personality and Social Psychology, 17,* 15–24.
17. Knapp, M. L., & Hall, J. H. (2002). *Nonverbal communication in human interaction.* Belmont, CA: Thomson Learning.
18. Mehrabian, A., & Williams, M. (1969). Nonverbal concomitants of perceived and intended persuasiveness. *Journal of Personality and Social Psychology, 13,* 37–58.
19. Foddy, M. (1978). Patterns of gaze in cooperative and competitive negotiation. *Human Relations, 31,* 925–938.
20. Hall. J. A. (1984). *Nonverbal sex differences: Communication accuracy and expressive style.* Baltimore: Johns Hopkins University Press.
21. Knapp, M. L., & Hall, J. H. (2002). *Nonverbal communication in human interaction.* Belmont, CA: Thomson Learning.
22. Byers, P., & Byers, H. (1972). Nonverbal communication and the education of children. In C. B. Cazden, V. P. John, & D. Hynes (Eds.), *Functions of language in the classroom.* New York: Teachers College Press.
23. Ickes, W. (1984). Compositions in black and white: Determinants of interaction in interracial dyads. *Journal of Personality and Social Psychology, 47,* 330–341.
24. Matsumoto, D. (2006). Culture and nonverbal behavior. In V. Manusov & M. L. Patterson (Eds.), *The Sage handbook of nonverbal communication* (pp. 219-235). Thousand Oaks, CA: Sage.
25. Akechi, H., Senu, A. Uibo, H., Kikuchi, Y. Hasegawa, T. & Hietanen, J. K. (2013). Attention to eye contact in the West and East: Autonomic responses and evaluative ratings. PLoS ONE, 8, e59312. https://www.ncbi.nlm.nih.gov/pubmed/23516627

CHAPTER 6: INDIVIDUAL GESTURES

Some Basic Ideas:

Gestures can reveal images in a person's mind and an understanding of how she sees and organizes her world.

Gestures reveal people's perceptions of the sizes, shapes, relative positions, and groupings of ideas, organizations, and people.

They also reveal perceptions of time, the order of things, bodily reenactments of an event, and references to ourselves and others.

People are most likely to gesture if they are enthusiastic and confident about a topic.

Gestures are a fascinating part of nonverbal communication. There are two types of gestures: *emblems* and *illustrators*. Emblems have meanings that are clearly articulated by the gesture, and people within a culture generally understand their meaning. Some examples of gestures are "Be quiet," "I don't know," "Good," and "OK." Below are photographs of these emblem gestures.

Gesture for "Be quiet"

Gest

ure for "I don't know"

Gesture for "Good"

Gesture for "OK" or "Good"

Emblems differ across cultures. For example, in the United States, the gesture above for "OK" means everything is good. However, in other cultures it can mean something completely different. In the 1950s when Richard Nixon was vice president, he went to Brazil. As he was getting off the plane, someone asked him how his trip had gone and he gave the gesture for "OK." Unfortunately in Brazil, this gesture is interpreted the way North Americans interpret holding up one's middle finger. The local newspaper printed a picture of Nixon giving this gesture to the country, and it wasn't well received.[1]

The other type of gesture is called an *illustrator*. Unlike emblems, illustrators don't have a specific meaning. Sometimes they are synchronous with speech, but at other times they show an image in a person's mind and reveal how she perceives her environment. The best example of gestures that reveal images are those that accompany directions. Ask someone to tell you how to get to a local landmark and watch her hands. Generally she will draw a visual image with her hands as she gives directions. These gestures reveal how far away she sees things and where you need to turn right or left.

Several years ago I was on a business trip driving in an unfamiliar area. I stopped a cabdriver and asked him to give me directions to a specific street. He told me to go down to the second light and then to take a left. When he made the gesture indicating how far to go down before taking a left, he extended his arm all the way from his body. I followed his directions and went down to the second light, which wasn't very far away. I remembered his gesture and recalled how he had extended his arm far away from his body, which told me that the second light was far away in his mind. I decided to go down one more light and then take a left. It was there that I found my street. It turns out that although his speech was not accurate, his gestures certainly were. They told me the second light was far away.

Gestures Facilitate Speech

One of the more interesting aspects of gestures is that they help people talk fluently. The fact that people use gestures even when they're on the telephone, which suggests that gestures serve a function beyond audience comprehension. Gesturing helps us find the right words and communicate thoughts, particularly when it's difficult to talk.[2,3] People gesture more when a cognitive task is difficult, when speaking a second language, and when they're being distracted by stimuli in the environment and need to concentrate.[4] Thus, gestures may actually help us to think and to process information around us. One theorist believes that gestures may help reduce our cognitive load while speaking.[5] Often people may be unaware that they're using gestures when they're speaking, but they would have more difficulty talking if they were unable to gesture. Thus, the increased use of gestures can tell us how difficult it is for a person to find the right words for something or how cognitively complex it is for them to talk.

Gestures help people talk.

I pay close attention when people start gesturing to find words. Their gesturing shows that they're having difficulty articulating their thoughts, which can be useful when I'm trying to understand concepts and feelings that are difficult to translate into words. Someone who is having difficulty putting something into words may not talk about that particular subject very often and may not have a ready description at hand. And, if I see a person gesturing fairly frequently to help themselves talk, that tells me this person has some articulation issues.

Gestures Reveal Sizes, Shapes, Relative Position, and Groupings

Often people indicate the sizes and shapes of things with their hands. Sometimes these gestures are made intentionally as a way of describing something. For example, when Mark says he "caught a fish this big ...," his accompanying gesture indicates the size of it for the audience's benefit. In other cases, however, people allude to the sizes or shapes of things without realizing that they are painting these portraits with their hands.

The sizes and shapes of things can be highly revealing in telling you about the actual sizes and shapes of objects in a person's environment, but it can also be revealing when people are talking about abstract ideas. If your colleague tells you that she has a big idea and makes a gesture that is very large, she is telling you how big she thinks this idea will be. In contrast, if your manager tells you that a colleague has a big idea and his gesture is relatively small, maybe he doesn't view it as a big idea after all. Or if someone says that he went around and around to find your office and his gesture reveals a frantic set of entangled circles, the gesture tells you what his path was like. Another person might tell you she went around and around, but her gesture shows two sets of clear circles. In this case, the words are the same but the two gestures tell you that one person's journey was totally different from the other's. The following pictures show examples of size and shape gestures. The first person shows the size of something, and the second person shows a shape.

A size gesture

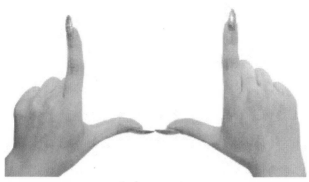

A shape gesture

People also indicate the relative position where two or more things reside with gestures and the space around their bodies. These gestures could be references to physical objects such as where a table is located relative to a couch, or they could refer to people and ideas. The most common gesture is to place your hands near each other as if you're holding something, and then place this object in a physical space. See the next picture for an example. This woman is placing something over to her right side. If she was to show you the relation of two things, her next gesture would do the exact same thing in a different physical space in front of her body. The difference between the two spaces reveals how far apart they're perceived to be. For example, imagine that Tammy tells you that she and her colleague, Christine, have different views on something. She uses her hands to place her view on the far-left side of her body and Christine's view all the way over on the far-right side of her body. Her gesture is telling you that the two viewpoints are far apart. In contrast, Gina may tell you that she and the CEO of her company have similar perspectives; she puts the two perspectives close to each other, which tells you how closely they reside in her mind. I always find it interesting when people don't tell you how close or far apart things are in their mind but reveal the distance with their gestures. Sometimes, I have discerned that someone perceives a wide discrepancy between himself and another person just by indicating where his viewpoint resides relative to the other person's viewpoint.

A gesture of where something resides in a physical or psychological space

Gestures also reveal how things are grouped. Because gestures reveal relative position, they tell you which things go together. As mentioned previously, people use the space in front of them to show you where things reside. The things that are closely aligned are placed next to each other or put in the same space. If you look at someone describing the various people in an organization, you can see how he perceives these individuals by seeing which ones he places together and which ones he places separately. I sometimes ask people to describe the various departments within their company and observe which ones are perceived as most allied by where they place the different departments around their body. Sometimes people will describe an organizational chart with their gestures and place people in various positions next to and on top of one another. The difference in status is revealed by the amount of space between individuals in the hierarchy.

Gestures Reveal Perceptions of Time

One of the more interesting uses of gestures is in communicating time. People sometimes reveal how long ago something happened or how far in the future they envision something occurring by where they place their hands relative to each other. Generally gestures about the future are made in front of a person and gestures about the past are made by motioning behind. A couple of gestures that people use to indicate the future involve holding one hand close to the body and then stretching the other one in front of that hand to indicate time passing between the two hands. I tell people to play close attention to a gesture when customers are talking about when they intend to make a decision about something. If one hand is stretched out very far from the other one, that decision will be made in the far future. But if the hand that is stretched out is fairly close to the other hand, that decision should be made fairly soon. I pay close attention to these gestures when dealing with potential clients who are telling me when they're likely to make a decision about awarding some work that I've proposed for them.

People also use gestures to refer to the past. Generally people will motion over their shoulder or motion backward as a way to indicate the past. Sometimes when people describe something that happened "a long, long time ago," they indicate how long ago by how far they motion behind them or how many times they make the backward motioning gesture. I like to watch how closely these time gestures match the words people use. If Lisa tells you that her company was started a long, long time ago, the gesture that accompanies this phrase should say the same thing. If it doesn't, it may indicate that her company wasn't started all that many years ago.

Gestures Reveal the Order of Things

Gestures also reveal the order in which people do things and the steps they take. One way that people indicate order is through counting gestures where they count off one, two, three, and so on. People will often grab a finger for the first step and then a finger for the next step until all steps have been described. The other way that people enact ordering is by apportioning the space in front of their bodies. The first step is indicated by taking the two hands as if they're holding something and indicating that some action occurs first by motioning to the left side of their body. The next step occurs just to the right of that space and so forth. Often people will indicate both the size of the step and the order of it by how far apart the hands are and where they put them in front of their body. So the first step will be shown in the left part of the space, the second step will be over to the right, and so on. If the first step is bigger than the second one, the hands may be farther apart for that first gesture than for the second one.

Gestures Reveal Bodily Reenactments

People also reveal how they do things, what exactly occurred, and what their experience is of things when they use gestures to replicate an incident. A good example is shown in the next picture where the person is showing how he punched a bully when he was a kid. Obviously the gesture is an example of a reenactment of the incident and his hands and facial expression tell us about his role in it. Gestures also reveal how people use things and what they did at each stage of the process. One of my favorite exercises that I use in workshops is to ask people to explain how they use an appliance such as a coffeemaker or washing machine. Immediately people start to gesture as they explain how make coffee. They will open an invisible cupboard, pull out a cup, put it on the counter next to the machine, pull out the filters, and so forth. You can see all the bodily reenactments, which can be fairly complicated if you look closely.

A gesture of a bodily reenactment

Gestures Reveal References to Ourselves and Others

People also gesture when they're referring to objects and to people. Pointing gestures are used to refer to people and things around us. When talking about people, we sometimes point quite overtly and at other times subtly. In the following pictures, the one on the left shows a man overtly pointing to someone or something. People also point very subtly to others who exemplify certain things. I've seen people describe a type of person and very subtly motion to someone who represents that type. Often they don't even realize they're motioning to that individual, but their gesture betrays their beliefs. One of my favorite examples occurred with a manager who was talking to a large group of people in his company. He was in the middle of a speech when he gestured to the group and said, "This is something that *we* should do." His gesture clearly indicated that he wanted the group to do something. He was not pointing to himself; he was pointing (and referring) to them.

The other thing people do with their gestures is reveal references to themselves and indicate beliefs that are highly important. The way people indicate important beliefs is by pointing to their chest or motioning toward themselves. One CEO I observed said to his audience, "This is something that we believe!" as he pointed to his heart. His gesture indicated that this belief is one that he holds near to his heart—quite literally. People also refer to themselves when they gesture. As you can see in the next picture, the woman is clearly pointing to herself and indicating that this discussion is about her.

Gesture referring to others

Gesture referring to oneself

Gestures Reveal Emotions, Enthusiasm and Confidence about a Topic

Gestures are most likely to occur when people have strong feelings about something. North Americans are most likely to gesture when they're angry, horrified, distressed, agitated or excited[6]. Thus, gestures occur when we have strong reactions. Gestures also tend to occur when we're enthusiastic about a topic or have a lot of confidence or knowledge about an area. Watch someone who is speaking, particularly a good public speaker, and you'll see that the words that are often emphasized with large gestures. The reason people tend to make larger gestures on these points is that gestures are synchronous with speech. One type of gesture that doesn't communicate an image, a reference, or a bodily reenactment is called a *baton* because it beats to the rhythm of our speech. Batons are naturally occurring gestures that we don't control. When people express a strong feeling in their speech, the resulting baton gesture is also strong.

People tend to gesture most when they're confident and enthusiastic about a topic and when they're not concerned about how they're being evaluated. People are less likely to gesture if they aren't knowledgeable about something or if they're worried about how they're coming across to others.[6] The woman in the next picture looks very confident, comfortable and enthusiastic about something. When people aren't confident about a topic or are worried about the impression they're giving, they gesture very little. I once did a workshop where we did an exercise on gestures. Each person had a partner except for one man. I went over and asked him if he wanted to do the exercise with me. He promptly told me that he doesn't gesture at all. We did the exercise and he never moved his hands. That is, until we started talking about a topic that wasn't part of the exercise—his kids. His hands began flying and he made numerous gestures. Obviously we had hit upon a topic that he was enthusiastic about and that he felt confident discussing.

Gestures reveal enthusiasm and confidence.

The Least You Need to Know

- Gestures can reveal images in a person's mind and an understanding of how a person perceives her world.
- Gestures can help us talk and find the right words.
- Gestures reveal how we see the size, shape, relative position, and groupings of objects, people, and organizations by where we place things relative to one another in the space around our bodies.
- Gestures reveal perceptions of time and how far in the future or past people perceive things occurring. These perceptions are revealed through the length of a gesture or the degree of motioning that represents the past or the future.
- Gestures also reveal how people see the order of things and how long each step takes by identifying which things occur first, second, and third in the space around them.

- o People reveal how they use things and their bodily experience of an event by using gestures to reenact an event.
- o We sometimes subtly and overtly refer to ourselves and others with pointing gestures.
- o People gesture the most when they are enthusiastic and confident about a topic.

Some Things to Think About

There are certain things you'll want to observe with gestures:

- o Do gestures match speech? If someone tells you that something is far away, or very old, does the gesture match what she's saying? If the gestures don't match, it may indicate that she's lying.
- o Which gestures are the largest? Watch the ideas or parts of a person's speech that are synchronous with the largest gestures. Those large gestures tell you about the importance of that part of speech for that person.
- o Some people gesture a great deal and others gesture very little. It's important to keep that in mind when interpreting someone's individual gestures.
- o What types of gestures do people use the most? Is a colleague primarily showing you visual images or is he describing things primarily in abstract ways? People who gesture a lot and lay things out for you visually are telling you that they're highly visual in their outlook on the world, and they will benefit from visual examples and arguments. People who gesture a lot of bodily reenactments are telling you that they are very tactile in their experience of the world.

Improving Your Ability to Read Gestures

Gestures reveal so many things that they're worth watching on a regular basis.

- o Try to speak without gestures, particularly when explaining something or persuading someone of a viewpoint that you know he or she doesn't hold. Note the effect that not being allowed to gesture has on your ability to talk.
- o Talk to someone else and ask him not to use any gestures of any kind in explaining or persuading you of something. Note the effect that not

gesturing has on his ability to speak. Note the effect that not gesturing has on your interest in what he's saying.

o   Record a professional speaker such as a politician giving a speech and notice if the words that are emphasized are the ones accompanied by the largest gestures.

o   Ask someone to describe some of the following things and watch his gestures. Discover content that the gesture reveals that his words don't. Have someone describe the following:

  o   How the first floor of his home is laid out
  o   How he gets from the front door of his home to his bedroom
  o   How to use an appliance in his home
  o   How he gets from his home to work
  o   A painting so that you could roughly reproduce it (without having the painting nearby)
  o   A vacation spot in detail

o   Watch when someone talks about something she is excited about or confident in discussing—does she tend to gesture more, less, or about the same?

o   Ask someone to describe different people or groups in an organization, or two different viewpoints, and discover how close this person perceives these people or viewpoints to be by observing where they are placed relative to one another.

References

1.   Richmond, V. P., & McCroskey, J. C. (2000). *Nonverbal behavior in interpersonal relations*. Needham Heights, MA: Allyn & Bacon.
2.   Chawla, P., & Krauss, R. M. (1994). Gesture and speech in spontaneous and rehearsed narratives. *Journal of Experimental Social Psychology, 30,* 580–601.
3.   Krauss, R., Morrel-Samuels, P., & Colasante, C. (1991). Do conversational hand gestures communicate? *Journal of Personality and Social Psychology, 61,* 743–754.
4.   Goldin-Meadows, S. (2003). *Hearing gesture: How our hands help us think.* Cambridge, MA: Belknap Press of Harvard University Press.
5.   Goldin-Meadows, S. (2003). *Hearing gesture: How our hands help us think.* Cambridge, MA: Belknap Press of Harvard University Press.

6. Ekman, P., & Friesen, W. V. (1969). The repertoire of nonverbal behavior: Categories, origins, usage and coding. *Semiotica*, *1*, 49-98.

7. Ekman, P., & Friesen, W. V. (1999). Hand movements. In L. K. Guerrero, J. A. DeVito, & M. L. Hecht (Eds.), *The nonverbal communication reader: Classic and contemporary readings* (2nd ed.). Prospect Heights, IL: Waveland Press.

CHAPTER 7: VOICE

Some Basic Ideas:

One's voice provides clues about one's age, gender, ethnicity, and social class.

The voice reveals when something is cognitively complex for a person. It can also reveal basic emotions.

You can also tell who wants to be like whom in conversations by observing the degree of voice modeling that occurs (who starts to sound like whom).

In many workplaces a great deal of communication doesn't occur in person. For some people, the majority of conversation with customers and colleagues occurs over the telephone. In my business, I've worked with an individual for many years and have never met him in person. I have no idea what he looks like, but I'm adept at reading his voice and identifying if he's having a good day or a bad one. Because so much communication occurs over the telephone, being able to read voices is an important part of nonverbal communication. However, when I say *voice*, I mean everything except speech—I am not referring to the content of what we say but rather to the other characteristics of our voices, such as the tone, pitch, speed of speech, and other attributes that reveal many things about us.

Voice Reveals Age, Gender, Social Class, Race, and Ethnicity

Our voices are like a fingerprint; they are unique. Each of us has specific voice qualities that differentiate us from others. Although we can disguise our voices, our specific voiceprint (called a spectrogram) can be readily recognized. Studies show that we're more than 90 percent accurate at recognizing the voices of people we know.[1] Our voices also reveal a multitude of other things—even our ages to within about five years.[2] Interestingly, we're more accurate at guessing how old people are when they're similar to us in age. We tend to hear those who are younger as being older and those who are older, we hear as younger. The reason age can be guessed fairly accurately is that the voice changes with age. Physical changes in the larynx and vocal cords that occur with age provide listeners with information about a person's age. In general, the pitch of our voices decreases from infancy through the teen years. And among men, pitch continues to decrease through middle age. After age eighty, pitch begins to increase among men. Among women, pitch doesn't change much in adulthood.

Not surprisingly, the voice also reveals the gender of a speaker about 96 percent of the time. Even when people whisper, you can accurately identify their gender about 76 percent of the time.[3] The reasons for this accuracy have to do with characteristics of the voice as well as the speech characteristics of men and women. Women have higher-pitched, softer voices than men. Men tend to be more monotonous in their speech, whereas women tend to have greater pitch variations and more rising and falling sounds when they talk. Women also tend to adhere to pronunciation standards better than men. Given that it isn't difficult to tell male from female voices, it's a major social blunder to mistake someone's gender. Thus, if the absolute pitch doesn't identify the person's gender, the other vocal characteristics should provide that information.

The voice also reveals one's social class, which is the class one belongs to as a result of education, income, and occupation. Americans tend to think about three classes: lower or working class, middle class, and upper class. Those in the lower class tend to be more polite and less confident, and tend to have more silent pauses, hesitations, and rising intonations. Their speech is characterized by less proficiency, less articulate speech, and less correct pronunciation of words than members of other classes.[4] You can determine a person's class just from the pronunciation of a single letter *r* in the word *fourth*. In a classic study of New Yorkers, researchers determined that pronouncing the letter *r* in words is highly correlated with class. The higher the social class, the more likely the person is to pronounce this letter.[5] This study has been repeated in England with a different set of pronunciations.

People can also distinguish between Caucasian and African American voices. In one study, listeners accurately identified white and black speakers 83 percent of the time.[6,7] It's possible that people are accurate because of differences in the voices of the two groups as well as speech and dialect differences. Voice also reveals one's ethnicity particularly when there are differences in pronunciation, fluency, and accents. It isn't difficult to tell an American southern accent from a foreign accent (such as French). However, it's sometimes difficult to pinpoint with accuracy where someone comes from originally.

Voice can also reveal one's culture. For example, how loudly one speaks varies by culture. Arabs and Latin Americans use higher voice volumes when speaking, whereas Asians and Europeans use lower volumes.[8,9,10] Another interesting difference is the use of silence. In general, Americans don't like silence in conversations; it makes them nervous. The presence of silence is perceived an indication that the interaction isn't going well. In contrast, cultures such as the Western Apache culture expect a large amount of silence, particularly in certain social situations.[11] Silence is the norm when interacting with strangers, when greeting people who have been away a long time, when responding to anger, and during mourning.

Knowing a person's age, gender, ethnicity, and social class is certainly useful if one knows very little about a person at the beginning of a telephone conversation. If you recognize that the person you're speaking with is a young woman in her twenties who comes from a working-class background, mentioning an opera star from the 1940s is probably going to be an ineffective way of connecting with her. Building rapport with another person often requires finding things in common and speaking about them. Talking about things that are unfamiliar doesn't increase comfort. I do many telephone interviews in my business and frequently have to connect with someone within a few seconds. I have to make a person feel comfortable, and then ask questions about whatever my project is about. With different age groups, I begin conversations with different topics that are hopefully appropriate to the person's age and gender, which helps to create rapport.

Voice Can Reveal Some Personality Attributes

Our voices can also reveal aspects of our personalities. Research in this area has shown that extroverted people tend to be moderately loud, fluent, slightly high-pitched, and dynamic, and to have longer utterances.[12] Research on the Type A personality, (known for being highly competitive, organized, ambitious, and impatient), has shown that this kind of person speaks loudly, quickly, emphatically, and dynamically.[13,14]

When interacting over the telephone, it's important to keep these personality differences in mind. Type A individuals tend to be impatient, they speak quickly, and they often like to talk with people who are similar to themselves in talking speed. I find that Type A individuals will finish the sentences of conversational partners who are speaking too slowly for them. Thus, I pay close attention to customers and colleagues and whether they're showing signs of extroversion or a Type A personality. If they show these signs, I'll modulate my speech so they feel comfortable talking to someone who has similar speech patterns.

Voice Reveals When Something Is Cognitively Complex

In addition to stable features of ourselves such as ethnicity and gender, the voice also reveals when someone is talking about something that is cognitively complex. Often speakers will say "um," "er," or "ah," or will pause while they figure out what they want to say.[15] Interestingly, speakers with larger vocabularies tend to have more of these filled pauses (such as *um, er*) because they have a larger database of words to search through to find the right word.[16] As a message becomes more complex, and as people pay more attention to the impression they're making, they tend to pause more in their communications.[17,18] The pause functions as a way for the speaker to find the right word, figure out an answer, or plan the next thing she wants to say. Strong emotions can also cause pauses in speech. For example, anxiety can cause a person to pause more, stutter, repeat words, and so forth. The pause can function as a way to get one's emotions under control.

I always listen for any type of pauses in the speech of those around me because they tell me when a person is experiencing some cognitive complexity or anxiety. When I first began looking for office space for my business, I interviewed several commercial real estate agents in Chicago. I remember asking several of them about the state of office space in the downtown area and listening for pauses. Several of the agents I interviewed didn't know their business well and started to make up facts, which were surrounded by pauses. The agent I eventually chose knew his market and his industry well, and it showed in his forthright answers and his lack of pausing. When I asked him tough questions, he demonstrated that my questions weren't too complex for him and didn't cause him any anxiety. He eventually found me office space in downtown Chicago on Michigan Avenue.

Voice Reveals Emotional States

Our voices also reveal the emotions we're experiencing. Through the voice, we're most able to identify the basic emotions of anger, sadness, happiness, fear, and contempt.[19] Apparently disgust is more difficult to identify just from the voice. We can tell emotions from more than just the words that are spoken; it's the pitch, speed, and intonation of the speech that indicates what people are feeling. Most of us can tell when a good friend or relative is having a bad day. We may not even know what we're responding to, but we can hear it in a person's voice. We also can decode emotions in strangers' voices. Apparently we're so adept at detecting emotional expressions from voices that we can distinguish things like hot anger and boredom from the voice alone.[20]

Emotions are an important thing to decode over the telephone because they provide us with an opportunity to connect with a person. It's generally a difference from normal speech that tips us off about what someone is feeling. When one of my customers called recently, I noticed that her speech was softer than normal, slower than usual, and punctuated by some sighs. I immediately knew she was sad even though she hadn't said anything about that to me. I asked her what was wrong and she replied that she didn't feel well. I said it sounded like she was sad and asked her if anything was wrong. She admitted she was sad about some things and that she had been having a hard time lately. The fact that I recognized what she was feeling helped me form a stronger connection with her.

Voice Reveals Deception

Because the voice reveals strong feelings, it can also reveal when someone is trying to be deceptive, but only if the person is nervous about being caught. These indicators are called leakage cues that tend to occur when the person wants to hide strong feelings, hasn't had time to rehearse the lie, and is worried about the consequences of being caught lying[21]. People who are deceptive tend to make more speech errors, have more unintentional pauses, speak for shorter periods of time and have a slower rate of speech than people who are honest. In addition, liars tend to have a higher pitch when they're lying[22]. So if you think someone is telling a lie about something, listen closely for speech errors, pauses, a slightly higher pitch and shorter answers compared to when you know they're answering honestly.

Voice Reveals Influence and Who Wants to Be Like Whom

One of the more intriguing parts of voice behavior relates to identification and modeling. People will adopt the speech patterns and voice qualities of those with whom they identify strongly and want to be like. This effect is called *speech convergence,* and it shows a typical pattern. Generally those who are lower in status tend to model those who are higher in status.[23] One of the more intriguing studies about this phenomenon was conducted by researchers who analyzed *Larry King Live* talk shows. They found that when Larry King interviewed higher-status guests such as George Bush, Bill Clinton, and Elizabeth Taylor, he changed his voice and converged more toward the higher-status person's way of speaking. When King was speaking with lower-status guests such as Dan Quayle, Gordon Sullivan, and Arthur Ashe, the guests tended to converge more toward his style of speaking.

Speech convergence is generally easy to recognize if you're familiar with a person's regular speech or if you know the accent for individuals from a specific region. One person with whom I work fairly regularly is originally from the United Kingdom. He has a fabulous English accent. Most of his associates, however, are from the Midwest. When he invites me to meetings at his firm, I can always tell which of his associates admire him the most by their speech. I've been at a couple of meetings where associates seem to acquire English accents that appear to get stronger as the meeting progresses.

Interestingly, speech convergence and turn taking in conversation is predictive of influence in organizations. Researchers have discovered that they can predict who has the greatest control over the information flow within an organization just by analyzing speech patterns. They analyzed how much individuals influence the speaking style of everyone they interacted with at work over several weeks. Individuals who had the strongest effect on the greatest number of people (in terms of their speaking style) were the ones who had the most control over the information flow within the organization.[24] Thus, when you identify which individuals have the most impact on others' speech, you are actually determining who has the most influence in an organization.

The Least You Need to Know

- Our voices are like a fingerprint. Each person has a unique voice that differentiates him or her from others.
- The voice reveals one's age, particularly people who are similar in age to us.
- One's voice reveals one's gender accurately about 96 percent of the time.
- Voice can also reveal one's social class, which is identified from speech patterns, proficiency in articulation, and pronunciations.
- Voice can also reveal if one is Caucasian or African American.
- Voice reveals some personality attributes such as extroversion.
- Our voices reveal when something is cognitively complex for us, which is shown when we pause or use non-fluencies such as *um* and *er*.

- The voice also reveals the basic emotions of anger, sadness, happiness, fear, and contempt. Emotions are transmitted through speed, pitch, and intonation.
- We tend to model the speech of those whom we like and want to be like. Those who are lower in status tend to adopt the speech of those who are higher in status.

Some Things to Think About

When thinking about the voice, it's useful to identify what the person's normal vocal pattern is and then to look at variations from that pattern. People differ in how quickly they speak, what emotions they express, and how influenced they are by others' speech around them. Thus, if Sarah normally talks slowly, take notice when her speech gets faster. Her faster rate of speech is telling you about her reaction to someone or something. Listen closely to the person's style of speech, pauses, pronunciations, and other paralinguistic qualities.

- Which emotions can you hear in the voice?
- What do the pauses reveal about the level of cognitive complexity she is experiencing and her desire to make a good impression?
- When do colleagues' speeches converge in meetings?
- Who is most likely to model whom and what does that say about the feelings of each person?

Improving Your Ability to Read the Voice

We often attend more to what people are saying than to how they're saying it. To improve your ability to read the voice, do the following:

- Listen to someone selling to you over the phone and see if you can guess her ethnicity, age, country of origin, and social class from her speech. What speech clues tell you each piece of information?
- Have someone say the following sentence: "I have to go now because I have something to do" several different times. Each time, have her express one of the basic emotions of happiness, anger, sadness, fear, surprise, disgust, and contempt. What vocal cues tell you that the person is expressing each emotion?

- Note when people pause during a discussion and what they seem to have trouble discussing. Is the topic cognitively complex for them or is it emotionally evocative?
- Listen to a drama without looking at it. What do the voices tell you about the different characters and what they're feeling and thinking?
- Record two people talking and notice if there is any speech convergence during the interaction. Record an interviewer who is talking with a higher-status person and a lower-status person and see what you hear. Does their speech converge at all? Whose speech converges?

References

1. Pittam, J. (1994). *Voice in social interaction: An interdisciplinary approach.* Thousand Oaks, CA: Sage Publications.
2. Hollien, H. (1987). "Old voices": What do we really know about them? *Journal of Voice, 1,* 2–17.
3. Lass, N. J., Hughes, K. R., Bowyer, M. D., Waters, L. T., & Broune, V. T. (1976). Speaker sex identification from voiced, whispered and filtered isolated vowels. *Journal of the Acoustical Society of America, 59,* 675–678.
4. Argyle, M. (1988). *Bodily communication.* Madison, CT: International Universities Press.
5. Labov, W. (1972). *Sociolinguistic patterns.* Philadelphia: University of Pennsylvania Press.
6. Lass, N. J., Tecca, J., Mancuso, R., & Black, W. (1979). The effect of phonetic complexity on speaker race and sex identification. *Journal of Phonetics, 7,* 105–118.
7. Walton, J. H., & Orlikoff, R. F. (1994). Speaker race identification from acoustic cues in the vocal signal. *Journal of Speech and Hearing Research, 37,* 738–745.
8. Hall, E. T., & Whyte, W. F. (1966). Intercultural communication: A guide to men of action. In A. G. Smith (Ed.), *Communication and culture.* New York: Holt, Rinehart & Winston.
9. Watson, O. M. (1970). *Proxemic behavior: A cross-cultural study.* The Hague, the Netherlands: Mouton.
10. Watson, O. M., & Graves, T. D. (1966). Quantitative research in proxemic behavior. *American Anthropologist, 68,* 971–985.
11. Basso, K. (1972). To give up on words: Silence in Western Apache culture. In P. Giglioli (Ed.), *Language in social context.* Harmondsworth, England: Penguin.

12. Scherer, K. R. (1978). Personality inference from voice quality: The loud voice of extroversion. *European Journal of Social Psychology, 8,* 467–487.

13. Friedman, M., Brown, A. E., & Rosenmann, R. H. (1969). Voice analysis test for detection of behavior pattern. *Journal of American Medical Association, 208,* 828–836.

14. Siegman, A. W. (1987). The telltale voice: Nonverbal messages of verbal communication. In A. W. Siegman & S. Feldstein (Eds.), *Nonverbal behavior and communication* (2nd ed.). Hillsdale, NJ: Lawrence Erlbaum.

15. Goldman-Eisler, F. (1968). *Psycholinguistics: Experiments in spontaneous speech.* New York: Academic.

16. Schachter, S., Christenfeld, N., Ravina, B., & Bilous, F. (1991). Speech dysfluency and the structure of knowledge. *Journal of Personality and Social Psychology, 60,* 362–367.

17. Christenfeld, N., & Creager, B. (1996). Anxiety, alcohol, aphasia and ums. *Journal of Personality and Social Psychology, 70,* 451–460.

18. Greene, J. O., & Ravizza, S. M. (1995). Complexity effects on temporal characteristics of speech. *Human Communication Research, 21,* 390–421.

19. Pittam, J., & Scherer, K. R. (1993). Vocal expression and communication of emotion. In M. Lewis & J. Haviland (Eds.), *The handbook of emotion.* New York: Guilford.

20. Banse, R., & Scherer, K. R. (1996). Acoustic profiles in vocal emotional expression. *Journal of Personality and Social Psychology, 70,* 614–636.

21. Ekman, P. (2001). Telling lies. New York: Norton.

22. Adler, R., B. & Proctor, R. F. (2017). *Looking out looking in.* Boston, Massachusetts: Cengage Learning

23. Giles, H., Mulac, A., Bradac, J. J., & Johnson, P. (1987). Speech accommodation theory: The next decade and beyond. In M. McLaughlin (Ed.), *Communication Yearbook 10.* Newbury Park, CA: Sage Publications.

24. Pentland, A. (2008). *Honest Signals: How they shape our world.* Cambridge, MA: MIT Press.

CHAPTER 8: EXISTENCE OF ADAPTORS

Some Basic Ideas:

Adaptors are small behaviors such as playing with one's hair or twirling a pen that occur in response to negative reactions that we have to ourselves or to others.

Adaptors also reveal when something is cognitively challenging.

Adaptors Reveal Negative Feelings about Ourselves or Others

The last part of PERCEIVE is the existence of adaptors. Adaptors are those small, fidgety behaviors that people do when they're stressed or bored. Examples of adaptors are biting one's lip, biting one's nails, twirling one's hair, playing with a necklace, or touching one's face. See examples of adaptors below.

Adaptor: biting one's lip

Adaptors: playing with one's hair

Adaptor: touching the face

The fascinating thing about adaptors is that we share them with primates. Monkeys show adaptors such as scratching, self-grooming, playing with sticks, or touching their faces when they encounter stressful situations. Ethologists see an increase in the number of adaptors when a monkey encounters a higher-status monkey, during territorial disputes, or when dealing with difficult decisions.[1] The following photos show some examples of monkeys exhibiting adaptors. The following picture looks very similar to the previous photo of the woman touching her face.

Monkeys showing adaptors

Adaptors fall into two groups: *self-adaptors* and *object adaptors*. Self-adaptors, as the name implies, involves manipulating a part of one's body such as twirling one's hair, touching one's face, biting one's lip, and so on. Object adaptors involve manipulating an object such as a ring, pencil, or cell phone. Some theorists believe that self-adaptors are a way of soothing oneself and that these behaviors give us a feeling of comfort that initially we received as children from our parents or guardians. Desmond Morris explains:

When we perform a self-intimacy we use part of the body as if it belonged to a comforting companion. During our infancy, our parents cuddle and hug us, and rock us gently back and forth if we are frightened or hurt. They pat us, stroke us, and caress us, and make us feel safe and secure, loved and wanted. When we are adults we often feel insecure and in need of gentle loving, but the parental arms are no longer there to protect us. Our own arms are there, however, and so we use them as substitutes.[2]

In general, adaptors are a response to negative reactions that we have to ourselves or to others. Among psychiatric patients, self-adaptors increase when a person's discomfort, anxiety, or depression increases.[4,5,6,7] Among more normal populations, stress tends to cause an increase in the number of adaptors that people show. In one study, researchers had participants watch one of two films. One film was unpleasant to watch and the other one was pleasant. The researchers then asked both groups to tell another person that the film was pleasant. Those who had seen the unpleasant film were being deceptive, which is stressful. The deceptive group displayed many more self-adaptors than the group that was telling the truth.[8]

Obviously a common adaptor that occurs all the time is engaging with one's smart phone. People have become increasingly comfortable with reaching for a smart phone during meetings or even friendly interactions. I've seen couples out at a restaurant who are more immersed in their cell phones than with one another. The increasing reliance on cell phones for information and connection makes them easy to reach for during other interactions. But this behavior is also an adaptor if it occurs during another interaction. And it indicates a level of boredom or stress, and potentially a desire to be somewhere else.

I always watch the number of adaptors that occur in meetings and when they tend to occur. In one meeting I attended, the number of adaptors started to increase as the meeting dragged on. I told the person who was managing the meeting that attendees were starting to become disengaged and he shifted to another topic. The change in nonverbal behavior was immediate. People leaned in closer to the table and stopped playing with pens, pencils, and cell phones. By changing the subject, the leader of the group changed the attendees' reaction to the meeting and the adaptors decreased. If you ever have to do a presentation to a group, notice if people start doodling, playing with pens, or doing other things. It's a sign that you're starting to lose your audience. By taking a break or changing the subject, you can reengage people. The change in the number of adaptors will be the proof.

Adaptors Reveal Cognitive Challenges

Adaptors are also more likely to occur when people are cognitively challenged. In one study, people were asked to read the names of colors that were sometimes printed in a contradictory color. For example, they would have to read the word *red* printed in green. This task can be challenging, particularly if one is trying to do it quickly. People who were reading the names of colors that were inconsistent with the printed color touched themselves more than when the two colors were consistent.[9] People also touched themselves more when they were answering questions about a reading they had just heard than when they were just listening to the passage.[10] Presumably, answering questions is more cognitively challenging than just listening to something. Thus, having a greater cognitive challenge can lead to more adaptors.

You can see how cognitively challenged those around you are when they're presenting information, facilitating a meeting, or managing an interaction. I tend to touch the ring on my right hand when I'm facilitating a group discussion. It's not that I'm particularly stressed, but I'm concentrating on what I'm doing and it's cognitively challenging to manage the group interaction. I'm listening to what people are saying, watching other people in the discussion, formulating new questions, and responding to what's been said already. My adaptors tend to occur when I experience the most challenge cognitively. That's probably the case for most people; as something becomes challenging or stressful, they start to exhibit more adaptors.

The Least You Need to Know

- Adaptors are small, fidgety behaviors that occur when people are stressed or bored. Examples include biting one's lip, biting one's nails, and touching one's face and hair.
- Adaptors fall into two groups: self-adaptors and object adaptors.
- Self-adaptors involve manipulating one's body such as touching one's hair or face.
- Object adaptors involve manipulating an object such as a pen, ring, or cell phone.
- Adaptors are most likely to occur in response to a negative reaction to oneself or others.
- Adaptors are also likely to occur when something is cognitively challenging. Tasks that are cognitively challenging are those that involve processing contradictory information (for example, saying the word *red* when it is printed in green) or that involve managing multiple tasks at once.

Some Things to Think About

Keep in mind that some people frequently display adaptors. In these cases, the *absence* of adaptors is more revealing than the presence of them. I once did a presentation to an advertising agency where a senior manager rocked back and forth the entire time. I asked him about it later and he said this behavior had just become a habit. He has a rocking chair in his office and one at his home, and he literally rocks all the time. The only time he doesn't rock back and forth is when he's really interested or really disturbed by something.

People also tend to have a favorite adaptor. As I mentioned previously, I tend to touch the ring on my right hand. You will see that people tend to resort to a few specific adaptors when they stressed or bored. Watch for these telltale signs. Some people also display adaptors frequently, whereas others don't. The presence of adaptors on a regular basis for a person may be indicative of their general level of stress.

Improving Your Ability to Read the Existence of Adaptors

Adaptors are often subtle and easy to miss. Being able to read adaptors requires simply being aware of what they are and when they tend to occur. Common object adaptors include

- playing with a pen or pencil;
- accessing a smart phone;
- playing with a napkin or piece of paper;
- playing with a straw, toothpick, pen, or other object in one's mouth;
- playing with a cell phone or personal digital assistant;
- doodling with a pen or pencil;
- playing with a necklace, ring, or other piece of jewelry;
- adjusting clothing.

Common self-adaptors include the following:

- Tapping one's fingers on a table
- Playing with one's hair
- Licking or biting one's lips continually
- Biting one's fingernails
- Stroking one's arms
- Touching one's face

If you want to become better at reading adaptors, start noticing these little behaviors and when they tend to occur.

- Record an interview in which the interviewer is asking contentious questions and notice if the person being interviewed shows any adaptors.
- Determine if the person knows that she is showing these behaviors.
- Identify if you have any specific adaptors and when they tend to occur to give yourself insight into their function.
- Notice how long you tend to exhibit adaptors and when you tend to stop.

References

1. Maestripier, D., Schino, G., Aureli, F., & Troisi, A. (1992). A modest proposal: Displacement activities as an indicator of emotions in primates. *Animal Behavior, 44,* 967–979.

2. Morris, D. (1977). *Manwatching: A field guide to human behavior.* New York: Harry N. Abrahms.

3. Ekman, P., & Friesen, W. V. (1972). Hand movements. *Journal of Communication, 22,* 353–374.

4. Freedman, N. (1972). The analysis of movement behavior during the clinical interview. In A. W. Siegman & B. Pope (Eds.), *Studies in dyadic communication.* New York: Pergamon Press.

5. Freedman, N., Blass, T., Rifkin, A., & Quitkin, F. (1973). Body movements and the verbal encoding of aggressive affect. *Journal of Personality and Social Psychology, 26,* 72–85.

6. Freedman, N., & Hoffman, S. P. (1967). Kinetic behavior in altered clinical states: Approach to objective analysis of motor behavior during clinical interviews. *Perceptual Motor Skills, 24,* 527–539.

7. Waxer, P. H. (1977). Nonverbal cues for anxiety: an examination of emotional leakage. *Journal of Abnormal Psychology, 86,* 306–314.

8. Ekman, P., & Friesen, W. V. (1974). Detecting deception from the body or face. *Journal of Personality and Social Psychology, 29,* 288–298.

9. Kenner, A. N. (1993). A cross-cultural study of body-focused hand movement. *Journal of Nonverbal Behavior, 17,* 263–279.

10. Heaven, L., & McBrayer, D. (2000). External motivators of self-touching behavior. *Perceptual and Motor Skills, 90,* 338–342.

CHAPTER 9: READING ELECTRONIC COMMUNICATIONS

Some Basic Ideas:

Electronic communications are on the rise and they lack important nonverbal information about the emotional reactions of others.

As a result, people are more likely to perceive others simplistically and stereotypically in electronic communications.

Emojis, photos and avatars have emerged to express emotions and can create a greater connection with people when used effectively.

Much Communication is Electronic

Over time, communication has become increasingly electronic in nature. Forms of communication that occur via email, texting, Instagram, Facebook, Twitter and LinkedIn are on the rise. According to the Pew report[1], 89% of Americans use the internet, 77% use a smartphone, and 69% use social media of some kind. Texting is particularly effective because 97% of tests are opened compared to 22% of emails and about 9 in 10 of text messages are opened within 3 minutes[2].

Perhaps that's why teenagers prefer texting over other forms of communication. Teens use texting for over half of their communications with friends followed by social media, especially when they own a smart phone, which the majority do[3]. This reliance on electronic communication, particularly among younger age groups has led to the creation of apps like 911.com that address the predisposition to communicate electronically. Older generations have a hard time imagining using an app for an emergency situation and wouldn't hesitate to dial 911, but younger age groups tend to feel most comfortable communicating via text.

How Electronic Communication Differs

Communications researchers discuss electronic communication in terms of "social presence," an awareness of another person that occurs in face-to-face interactions. Social presence is missing from written forms of electronic communication because we can't see the facial expression, hear the voice, and see the body language of the person with whom we're communicating. The resulting exchange is often more task oriented and less spontaneous[4]. It's possible task orientation occurs because people are less distracted by the nonverbal cues or because there isn't as much to decode except for the message itself.

People tend to be less inhibited in their electronic communications and to say things they wouldn't say in person[5]. Part of the reason for this is because there is no immediate emotional response to one's communications—one doesn't see the look of shame, sadness or embarrassment on the person who is receiving the communication. This disinhibition can be seen in the harsh commentary people have for individuals they don't know on platforms like Facebook. It's also shown in other ways. People who are trying to get to know one another via electronic communications tend to do so by asking personal questions[6] and revealing things they might not say in person. Apparently people feel less shy on the internet than in face-to-face encounters[7].

Research has found people mistakenly believe they're quite able to communicate sarcasm, anger, and sadness electronically[8]. Unfortunately, most of us overestimate our abilities in this area. This means that text, email and social media are not the ideal medium for conveying complex emotion.

Electronic Communicators More Likely to be Stereotyped

Because electronic communication is stripped of a variety of nonverbal cues, text-based communicators tend to be perceived more simplistically and more intensely. There is so little information in the content of the interaction, that texters fill in the blanks of their judgements with stereotypes[9]. This phenomenon occurs most often when people are interacting electronically for the first time. In one study, researchers told individuals they would be interacting with a person who was described as either intelligent or unintelligent. People were more likely to perceive an individual as similar to their expectations when they communicated over email than when talking on the telephone[10]. A similar result has been found for racial bias. When people believe they're speaking to an Asian woman versus an African American woman, they have more stereotypical perceptions of the woman after an email interaction than a telephone one[11].

Emojis, Photos & Avatars

The rise of emojis (e.g., ☐, ☺) may be partially in response to the limitations of email and texting. Emojis, bracketed expressions (e.g., <frown>, <smile>), qualifying statements (e.g., just kidding!) or abbreviations LOL (laugh out loud) supply context and personalize interactions. They can make stilted communication feel less formal and make the cold medium of a text message feel a little warmer. The most frequently used emojis are happy faces followed by sad faces, hearts and hand gestures[12]. Emojis are effective at expressing feelings that are complex and difficult to describe (such as the laughing-crying emoji), and to communicate inside jokes. Friends and romantic partners often infuse certain emojis with personally specific meaning as a playful way to build a shared visual vocabulary. Emojis can also be an easy way to deceive others given that it's easy to send over an emoji than it is to respond truthfully by text.

Photos serve as another way to create a greater feeling of social presence in electronic communications. Interestingly, the presence of a digital photo with an email request leads to greater acquiescence to a request than the same request without the person's photo[13]. Photos convey a tremendous amount of personal information. In one study researchers were able to deduce information about relationships, interests, hobbies, important causes, and personality attributes simply from studying Facebook profile photos[14]. Although this is one area where there are measurable gender differences. Men tend to select pictures that identify risk-taking behavior or status via clothing and objects whereas women tend to have profile photos that depict emotional expressions and family relationships[15].

Avatars are perhaps the most multidimensional way people can communicate electronically and they often mirror the way people behave in face-to-face encounters. Avatars can even mimic one another's expressions, leading to greater empathy and affinity between the communicators[16]. Interestingly, our avatars act much like we do in our offline interactions. Males tend to keep greater distances from others and to make less eye contact than females[17]. And female avatars express more emotion, make more apologies and use more tentative language than male avatars[18]—even when the person behind the avatar isn't the same gender as their avatar. Cultural differences also show themselves in avatar interactions with Asians keeping greater distances from other avatars than those from European countries[19].

The Least You Need to Know

- Much communication occurs electronically and is devoid of nonverbal information that's helpful to understand the feelings of the communicator.
- People are more confident of their ability to transmit emotional information via electronic means than they should be. Speaking over the telephone is a more accurate way to convey emotional information than through text alone.
- People are disinhibited in electronic communications and likely to say things that are overly harsh or personally revealing because they don't see the nonverbal reactions of those they're communicating with electronically.
- People tend to perceive those they interact with electronically as being more simplistic and stereotypical than they are as a result of the lack of rich information conveyed over the phone or in face-to-face encounters.
- Emojis, photos and avatars are tools that can be used to convey greater social presence and emotional information. The usage of them can create a stronger sense of the individual person. Avatars actually mimic some of the nonverbal behavior that occurs offline.

Some Things to Think About

As electronic communications replace so much of our in-person interactions, we must be aware of how our communications may be perceived. Conversely, we should take care to avoid simplistic and stereotypical perceptions of others. This means being mindful of how we communicate emotion, enthusiasm, liking and sarcasm when we email, text and post online.

When interacting with others electronically, keep in mind cultural and gender display differences. Be aware that people are less inhibited in their communications that occur, particularly on social media. People are likely to be showing a side of themselves they would never display in face-to-face interactions.

What kind of a person are you in electronic communications?

Improving Your Ability to Read Electronic Communications

In order to read electronic communications effectively, consider what information is <u>not</u> being conveyed.

- Make sure to ask questions and be aware of your own biases.
- When interacting over social media remember there is a public self that is being conveyed electronically and try to see beyond this presentation.
- Take time to think about how a piece of text can be interpreted differently when read with different tones of voice. Read important emails aloud to yourself with several different tones before sending. Clarify anything potentially ambiguous by adding qualifiers or emojis,
- Be careful about reading a tone into communications that isn't intended by the sender. Ask questions before drawing conclusions about the individual's feelings and intentions.
- Be aware of changes in individual style, but don't jump to conclusions. Someone who uses a lot of flowery language and suddenly becomes terse may not be feeling good, may be upset, or could be in a hurry.

References

1. Hitlin, P. (2018). Internet, social media use and device ownership in U.S. have plateaued after years of growth. Pew Research Report. https://www.pewresearch.org/fact-tank/2018/09/28/internet-social-media-use-and-device-ownership-in-u-s-have-plateaued-after-years-of-growth/
2. Connectmogul (2013, March 22). Texting statistics. http://connectmogul.com/2013/03/texting-statistics/
3. Anderson, M. (2015) How having a smartphone (or not) shapes the way teens communicate. Pew Research Report. https://www.pewresearch.org/fact-tank/2015/08/20/how-having-smartphones-or-not-shapes-the-way-teens-communicate/
4. Argyle, M. 1988. Bodily Communication. London, England: Methuen.
5. Donn, J. E. & Sherman, R. C. (2002). Attitudes and practices regarding the formation of romantic relationships on the internet. *Cyberpsychology and behavior, 5*, 107-123.
6. Tidwell, L. C., and Walther, J. B. (2002). Computer-mediated communication effects on disclosure, impressions, and interpersonal

evaluations: getting to know one another a bit at a time. *Human Communication Research, 28,* 317–348.

7. Knox, D., Daniels, V., Sturdivant, L. & Zusman, M. E. (2001). College student use of the internet for mate selection. *College Student Journal, 35,* 158–160.

8. Kruger, J., Epley, N., Parker, J, & Ng, Z. (2005). Egocentrism over e-mail: Can we communicate as well as we think we can? *Journal of Personality and Social Psychology, 89,* 925–936.

9. Walther, J. B. (1996). Computer-mediated communication: Impersonal, interpersonal, and hyperpersonal interaction. *Communication Research, 23,* 3–43.

10. Epley, N., & Kruger, J. (2005). When what you type isn't what they read: The perseverance of stereotypes and expectancies over e-mail. *Journal of Experimental Social Psychology, 41,* 414–422.

11. Epley, N., & Kruger, J. (2005). When what you type isn't what they read: The perseverance of stereotypes and expectancies over e-mail. *Journal of Experimental Social Psychology, 41,* 414–422.

12. Goldsborough, M. (2014). Putting your emotions on screen. *Teacher Librarian, 43,* 64.

13. Gueguen, N. & Jacob, C. (2002). Social presence reinforcement and computer mediated communication: The effect of the solicitor's photograph on compliance to a survey request made by e-mail. Cyberpsychology and Behavior, *5,* 139–142.

14. Wu, Y. J., Chang, W. & Yuan, C. (2015). Do Facebook profile pictures reflect users' personality? *Computers in Human Behavior, 51,* 880–889.

15. Tifferet, S., & Vilnai-Yavetz, I. (2014). Gender differences in Facebook presentation: An international randomized study. *Computers in Human Behavior, 38,* 388–399.

16. Fabri, M., Moore, D., & Hobbs, D. (2005, September). Empathy and enjoyment in instant messaging. In L. McKinnon, O. Bertelsen, & N. Bryan-Kinns (Eds.), *Proceedings of the 19ᵗʰ British HCI Group Annual Conference,* Edinburgh, England.

17. Yee, N., Bailenson, J. N., Urbanek, M., Chang, F, & Merget, D. (2007). The unbearable likeness of being digital: The perseverance of nonverbal social norms in online virtual environments. *Cyberpsychology and Behavior, 10,* 115–121.

18. Palomares, N. A., & Lee, E. (2010). Virtual gender identity: the linguistic assimilation to gendered avatars in computer mediated communication. *Journal of Language and Social Psychology, 29,* 5–23

19. Hasler, B. S., & Friedman, D. A. (2012). Sociocultural conventions in avatar-mediated nonverbal communication: A cross-cultural analysis of virtual proxemics. *Journal of Intercultural Communication Research*, *41*, 238-259.

CHAPTER 10: PUTTING IT ALL TOGETHER

Some Basic Ideas:

When observing others, pay special attention to three things: 1) variations from a person's normal behavior, 2) variations from the normative situation, and 3) variations with different people. These deviations reveal how people are responding to individuals and situations.

PERCEIVE tells us about engagement, liking, emotions, and the type of relationship between two people.

If you want to master PERCEIVE, learn each part of the system independently so you are proficient in each aspect. Reading all parts of nonverbal communication will come naturally after learning each part well.

O nce you know the different parts of PERCEIVE, you can begin putting them together. Each part of this system provides you with information about nonverbal communication that gives insight into what a person is thinking and feeling.

Some General Rules to Follow

When observing people, there are some general rules that I follow:
- Observe variations from a person's normal behavior.
- Observe variations from the situation.
- Observe variations across different people.

Each person has a baseline for what's normal for them. For example, some people are highly expressive and outgoing much of the time. Others are more introverted and less expressive. When observing people I try to gauge the baseline for that person. If Cathy is normally somewhat inexpressive but is particularly expressive in our interaction, her deviation from her normal behavior is indicative that something is going on with her. By reading all of her nonverbal behavior and factoring in her usual inexpressiveness, I have a great deal of information about her reaction to our interaction.

I also observe variations from the situation. Most situations have normative behavior associated with them. It would be highly unusual to laugh and be joyful at a funeral. In contrast, it would be highly unusual to be grief-stricken at an amusement park. Cultures have normative expectations for how to behave in different situations. If your manager typically has somber department meetings, it would be inappropriate to crack jokes and be amusing during these meetings. In contrast, a whole different set of behaviors might be expected for the company party. When watching people, I look for variations from the normative situation that has evolved among a group of people. So if a group discussion has evolved into a jovial event, I take that into account when I observe people's reactions to one another. Expressions of joy among this group may say more about the situation than about their feelings for one another. In contrast, if a situation is deadly dull, positive expressions in reaction to something would be highly revealing because they're at odds with the circumstances.

The last thing I observe is variations across different people. If Mark isn't particularly expressive with his colleagues but is very expressive with Karl, that behavior tells me something. It's his nonverbal behavior with various people and the deviations from it that tell me how he feels about Karl. Clearly he has a strong reaction to Karl. People are differentially communicative with different people, and their behavior tells you a great deal about how they feel about specific individuals.

PERCEIVE can be used to discern engagement, liking, emotions, and the type of relationship two people are having. I now discuss each of these areas and the nonverbal cues for each one.

PERCEIVE Tells about Engagement

Nonverbal communication provides information about how engaged people are with each other and with the events around them. The major indicators of engagement are the person's proximity, orientation, eye behavior, and existence of adaptors. People who are engaged and interested in a conversation with another person tend to *increase* their proximity (move closer) to the person and to orient directly toward that person. Another indicator of engagement is eye behavior. When we're interested in someone or something, we look more frequently and for longer durations than when we aren't interested. The last indication that a person is engaged is the lack of adaptors. When we become bored or stressed, we display adaptors. Thus, the lack of these adaptors along with other behaviors is a sign of engagement.

PERCEIVE Tells about Liking

You can tell the degree of liking that people have for others from their nonverbal behavior. The indicators of liking are the proximity, orientation, expressions, and eye behavior. As mentioned previously, we stand and sit near people we like and tend to orient directly toward these individuals. Our expressions, particularly our microexpressions, reveal our momentary reactions to people. When we don't like someone, we betray our feelings with those momentary microexpressions of contempt, irritation, and anger. Eye behavior is another strong clue to liking. We generally don't look at people we don't like. Thus, you can gauge liking from the amount of time people look at one another and their proximity, orientation, and positive expressions.

PERCEIVE Tells about Relationships between Others

Nonverbal behavior also reveals liking, status and the closeness of a relationship between two people. The best way to identify the level of closeness is to observe how closely the two people sit or stand, how much they look at each other, and how much they touch one another. Close relationships have more of all of these behaviors. Nonverbal behavior also reveals status. You know who the leader is in a meeting because of where she sits, how much people look at her, how people are oriented toward her, and how attentive they are when she talks. In general, higher-status people command more nonverbal attention than lower-status people. You can also tell differentials in status by a person's level of approachability. The more approachable a person tends to be, the lower her status. Generally people are less likely to approach a high-status person, less likely to engage her for a long time, less likely to touch her, and so on.

PERCEIVE Tells about Emotions

Nonverbal behavior tells us a great deal about other people's emotional experiences. Expressions, particularly microexpressions, reveal the momentary reactions people have to one another and to the situations they encounter. Those momentary expressions are true, uncontrolled responses that reveal what a person is experiencing internally from minute to minute. The voice also indicates the emotions that people are experiencing. We are quite adept at detecting the emotions from the voice alone, and we know the telltale signs of nervousness, joy, fear, sadness, and so on just from listening to someone speak.

PERCEIVE Is Useful for Reading Customers and Colleagues

Because you can gain insight into so many areas of another person, reading nonverbal communication is invaluable in professional situations when you're trying to understand customers and colleagues. I use these skills all the time. One example occurred when I was meeting with a potential client. He started the meeting by sitting catty-corner to me and was almost turned away from me. His orientation was completely off from the start. I saw this behavior immediately and realized he wasn't interested in a business relationship. So instead of talking about what I intended to discuss, I started asking him about his business and how things were going for him. He started to become more engaged in the conversation and began to orient toward me. As he started to brag about a recent success, he oriented directly toward me and moved himself closer. I saw my opportunity to introduce the topic I wanted to discuss. As I began talking, he showed a microexpression of sadness. It was then that I started to think that maybe he was having issues in his business. I mentioned that the business climate had been a little tough lately and he agreed very strongly, showing several more microexpressions of sadness. I realized that he was in no position to start a professional relationship and that he was struggling with his current business. I stopped pursuing the original discussion and just focused on him and his current issues. At the end of the meeting, he told me he had really enjoyed talking and looked forward to potentially doing work together. Because I had been sensitive to his nonverbal behavior and reacted to what was going on, he had a positive reaction to me. He did a project with me several months later. My ability to read him and respond appropriately turned a potentially difficult situation into an opportunity.

Improving Your Ability to PERCEIVE

The best way to improve your ability to read nonverbal communications is to learn each part of PERCEIVE individually. Attempting to learn all aspects of nonverbal communication at once is overwhelming. Begin by familiarizing yourself with each piece of PERCEIVE and then practice reading that one until it becomes second nature to you. As you master each part, you can begin to add another part of PERCIEVE and then integrate these parts. The result is that you will learn to read *all* of nonverbal communication easily and it will become something you do automatically.

One way to read nonverbal behavior better is to spend more time watching people and less time listening to them. In North American culture, we spend a lot of time listening to what people say and analyzing the content of their words. Spend time just watching instead. Watch people on the bus, in meetings, and at social events. Being able to observe people without being able to hear them will help you to *see* their nonverbal behavior rather than reacting to their words. Just watch and determine as much as you can about what people are thinking and feeling. Test your observations as much as possible. When I go to a wedding, I like to watch people and guess which couples are happy and which ones aren't. I'm often correct in my assessments.

And as mentioned in the first chapter, another great way to improve reading nonverbal communication is to watch movies and watch them without any sound. Because we rely so heavily on listening to the words, this approach will force you to watch the nonverbal behavior. Watch movies that you haven't seen before and look at the first 10 to 20 minutes. Try to determine how people think and feel about one another and what type of relationship they're having. Then go back and watch the portion that you observed with the volume turned up. See how much you were able to deduce just by watching their nonverbal behavior. You will become better and better at this over time.

CONCLUSION

You selected this book because you have an interest in reading the hidden communications around you. You now realize that these communications are not hidden at all. They're right out there in the open and accessible to everyone. Our bodies transmit messages nonverbally in many different ways. And as I said earlier, people can choose not to speak, but they can never be silent nonverbally. We are always communicating something. It's unfortunate that we're never taught how to read body language, given how useful it is in so many situations. We can see how people think and feel, along with the way they relate to others around them. If we had been taught this basic skill growing up, there would probably be fewer misunderstandings and more honesty in our interactions.

As you become more adept at reading others with PERCEIVE, you'll begin to see nonverbal communication everywhere. You will read the proximities and orientations of those you interact with, see microexpressions, and read aspects of voices. You'll be able to read people's gestures and ascertain where their eyes focus and for how long. You'll know what adaptors mean and how to read physical contact. All of these things will allow you to read people and to respond appropriately. Your responses will then elicit other reactions from those you observe, which will help you understand a particular person or situation. As you continue to read people, you'll understand some individuals intimately and begin to have a good understanding of particular groups and organizations. All of this information provides you with a unique insight into the people in your professional life.

As you learn to read others better, think about your own nonverbal communication and what it reveals about you. All of the things that you see in others are things that other people may see in you. For example, the people you don't like may get less eye contact from you and you may stand farther away from them. Some people read body language intuitively and may get a *feeling* that you don't like them. You may want to think about what you convey and how you can use your nonverbal communication to convey certain messages about yourself. Do you want to appear likeable? Do you want to appear competent? Do you want to appear thoughtful? What are the nonverbal behaviors that you associate with people who have these qualities? How can you use these nonverbal communications to your advantage? Learning to read nonverbal communication tends to engender a better understanding of our own nonverbal communication and how we can use it to our benefit.

You now have a language that you can understand and use in your professional life. Like most second languages, it may be difficult to learn at first, but it's well worth being fluent in it. I wish you much success in reading and using nonverbal communications.

ABOUT THE AUTHOR: ANNE E. BEALL

Anne E. Beall is the founder and CEO of Beall Research, Inc. She specializes in strategic market research and was previously at The Boston Consulting Group (BCG). During her tenure at BCG, Beall directed market research for the Chicago office. She specializes in leveraging frameworks and concepts from psychology to market research and has particular expertise in the area of emotions.

Beall conducts both qualitative and quantitative market research. She specializes in conducting large-scale, complex strategic studies for Fortune 500 companies. She has conducted research on brand positioning and brand equity, determinants of customer loyalty and switching behavior, development of new product concepts, extendibility of brands, launches of new products and services, pricing, and segmentations of consumers and businesses. She has worked in a variety of industries, including food, beverages, telecommunications, insurance, brokerage firms, utilities, package transportation and delivery, retail, schools, hospitals, foundations, furniture, and personal-care products.

Beall has conducted hundreds of in-depth interviews, focus groups and surveys across many industries. She specializes in analyzing what respondents say and, more important, what they don't say. She has an unusual sensitivity for people and has created a method for reading nonverbal behavior called PERCEIVE, which can be used to read respondents when they are unable or unwilling to express their thoughts and feelings.

Beall has written book chapters and articles about consumer psychology and marketing. She has published the following books: *Strategic Market Research: A Guide to Conducting Research that Drives Businesses, Cinderella Didn't Live Happily Ever After: The*

Hidden Message in Fairy Tales, Heartfelt Connections: How Animals & People Help One Another, Community Cats: A Journal Into the World of Feral Cats, and *The Psychology of Gender.*

Beall received her MS, MPhil, and PhD degrees in social psychology from Yale University. In her spare time she runs, fosters stray cats for various shelters in Chicago, and enjoys the many restaurants of the city.

Made in the USA
Middletown, DE
25 May 2019